T0301781

Fostering Monetary & Financial Cooperation in East Asia

World Scientific Studies in International Economics
(ISSN: 1793-3641)

7 World Scientific
Studies in
International
Economics

Fostering Monetary & Financial Cooperation in East Asia

Editors

Duck-Koo Chung
North East Asia Research Foundation, South Korea

Barry Eichengreen
University of California, Berkeley, USA

World Scientific

NEW JERSEY · LONDON · SINGAPORE · BEIJING · SHANGHAI · HONG KONG · TAIPEI · CHENNAI

Published by

World Scientific Publishing Co. Pte. Ltd.

5 Toh Tuck Link, Singapore 596224

USA office: 27 Warren Street, Suite 401-402, Hackensack, NJ 07601

UK office: 57 Shelton Street, Covent Garden, London WC2H 9HE

Library of Congress Cataloging-in-Publication Data

Fostering monetary and financial cooperation in East Asia / edited by Duck-Koo Chung & Barry Eichengreen.

    p. cm. -- (World scientific studies in international economics, ISSN 1793-3641 ; v. 7)

    Includes bibliographical references and index.

    ISBN-13: 978-9814271530

    ISBN-10: 9814271535

    ISBN-13: 978-9814271547

    ISBN-10: 9814271543

    1. East Asia--Economic integration. 2. East Asia--Economic policy. 3. East Asia--Foreign economic relations. I. Chung, Duck-Koo, 1948– II. Eichengreen, Barry J.

    HC460.5.F67 2009

    332'.042095--dc22

                          2009007819

British Library Cataloguing-in-Publication Data

A catalogue record for this book is available from the British Library.

Typeset by Stallion Press

Email: enquiries@stallionpress.com

Printed in Singapore.

Acknowledgments

The project of which this volume is the product received the support of a number of generous donors: the North East Asia Research Foundation, the Korean Ministry of Finance and Economy, the Korea International Economic Policy Institute, Kookmin Bank, Shinhan Bank, Chosum Ilbo, and Maeil Business Newspaper. In addition, Yeongseop Rhee of Sookmyung Women's University helped in coordinating the project. We are grateful to them all.

Contents

List of Figures

List of Tables

Contributors

Hee-Yul Chai
Department of Economics
Kyonggi University, South Korea

Duck-Koo Chung
Chairman
North East Asia Research Foundation, South Korea

Paul De Grauwe
Department of Economics
Catholic University of Leuven, Belgium

Barry Eichengreen
Department of Economics
University of California, Berkeley, USA

Motoshige Itoh
Department of Economics
University of Tokyo, Japan

Masahiro Kawai
Asian Development Bank Institute, Japan

Woosik Moon
Graduate School of International Studies
Seoul National University, South Korea

Yeongseop Rhee
Department of Economics
Sookmyung University, South Korea

Deok Ryong Yoon
Research Fellow
Korea Institute for International Economic Policy, South Korea

Yongding Yu
Institute of World Economics and Politics
Chinese Academy of Social Sciences, China

CHAPTER 1
Introduction

Duck-Koo Chung and Barry Eichengreen

The importance of monetary and financial cooperation is a prominent theme in economic policy discussions in East Asia. Hardly a day goes by without a call by a central bank governor, finance minister, or any other official for closer collaboration in strengthening financial markets and fostering exchange-rate stability. Moving from words to deeds, the last decade has seen, among other measures, the Chiang Mai Initiative (CMI) of emergency financial supports and the Asian Bond Market Initiative (ABMI) to build more active and liquid bond markets.

From the perspective of North America, this emphasis is striking. The national economies of North America, like the national economies of East Asia, have become more interdependent, both economically and financially, with the reduction in transportation and communications costs and the expansion of intraregional trade and financial flows. North America is ahead of East Asia in building a free trade area, having signed the North American Free Trade Agreement (NAFTA) in 1994, where the ASEAN countries aim at completing their economic community only in 2015. But despite the expansion of trade and investment flows within North America, there is little perception of an urgent need to deepen monetary and financial cooperation. The US dollar, Canadian dollar, and Mexican peso float independently. There is no overt effort to coordinate monetary policies. The three countries regulate their financial markets independently. In all these respects, the contrast with East Asia is stark.

There are four explanations for why Asia is different or at least aspires to be so. First is the region's economic structure and strategy. In terms of strategy, Asian policymakers have long valued exchange-rate stability. The highly successful Asian model of the second half of the 20th century emphasized exports as an engine of growth and development. It saw stable

1

exchange rates as valuable, even essential, for fostering the growth of export industries. Once upon a time, this meant the stability of exchange rates vis-à-vis Asia's principal extra-regional market. In other words, it meant stabilizing currencies against the US dollar. But with the growth of intraregional trade — both in parts and components as Asia elaborates regional production networks and in final goods as consumer demand rises with living standards — it has also come to mean the stability of exchange rates among the region's currencies themselves.

A second explanation is the financial crisis of 1997–98. The crisis revealed the deficiencies of prevailing monetary and financial arrangements. Pegging to the dollar exposed Asian countries to a deterioration in competitiveness if the dollar rose against the yen, as was the case in the mid-1990s. Moreover, pegging unilaterally might become prohibitively expensive or even technically impossible as the liquidity of international financial markets and the volume of international capital flows continued to rise, a reality revealed by the helplessness of Asian governments and central banks in the face of capital flight in 1997. Another lesson of the crisis was that the underdevelopment of local financial markets led to an excessive reliance on bank intermediation, creating too-big-to-fail and connected-lending problems. It led to overdependence on short-term foreign-currency debt, giving rise to the financial vulnerabilities associated with currency and maturity mismatches.

The conclusions drawn included the need for a monetary policy set with Asian conditions in mind, not one decided by the Federal Reserve Board as prevailed when Asian currencies were pegged to the dollar. They included the need for collective approaches to stabilizing exchange rates. They included the importance of working to develop regional bond markets, collectively as well as individually insofar as only a region-wide bond market would possess the scale and liquidity to compete with extra-regional financial markets and centers.

A third factor encouraging these initiatives is the greater financial resources now available for their pursuit. Asia is the world's fastest growing region, and as it has grown it has accumulated more wealth to be allocated via financial markets. More to the point, as a result of shifting from current account deficit before the crisis to current account surplus subsequently, the region has accumulated massive international reserves. Some part of these reserves can be allocated to the Asian Bond Fund (ABF) to help develop an integrated regional bond market. Another part can be committed to the CMI and thereby be made available to neighboring countries in financial need.

A final explanation is the desire for self-reliance and the growing self-confidence that come with strong economic performance. Asian countries were not happy with the hard line of the US Treasury and the International Monetary Fund (IMF) when the crisis forced them to seek financial assistance. Depreciation of the dollar in 2003–07 and the turmoil in US credit markets in 2007–08 did not enamor them of an international system in which the dollar was the main form of international reserves and the United States set the tone for global financial affairs. Better, they concluded, was to invest in developing a more autonomous regional monetary and financial system through which East Asian countries could provide the necessary functions for themselves.

The last 10 years have seen considerably more progress in the financial than the monetary sphere. In finance, there has been the CMI for emergency finance assistance. Established in 2000 as a collective endeavor of the 10 Association of East Asian (ASEAN) nations together with China, Japan, and South Korea (known collectively as the ASEAN+3 grouping), the CMI provides a network of bilateral swaps and repurchase agreements through which countries can obtain emergency assistance. Chapter 3 by Chai and Yoon describes and analyzes these developments in detail.

There has also been the ABMI and the ABF to develop regional debt markets. The ABMI, also an initiative of ASEAN+3, focuses on developing a stronger bond-market infrastructure, relying on the analysis and findings of regional study groups. The ABF, an initiative of the Executives' Meeting of East Asian and Pacific Central Banks (a grouping that includes not just East Asia but also Australia and New Zealand), seeks to foster the participation of investors on those markets by creating a Pan Asia Bond Index Fund, a passively managed fund administered by private-sector managers, and a series of dedicated national index funds.

Both sets of initiatives have continued to evolve. Participants in the CMI have committed to transforming their scheme into a regional reserve pool capable of being deployed all at once in the event of need. They have taken steps to create a surveillance mechanism designed to identify financial vulnerabilities, call for corrective action, and monitor the adequacy of the steps taken in response. Better information on the causes of financial difficulties and on how governments are responding to them, of the sort that can be assembled through such surveillance, should help members of the CMI to determine when activation is appropriate and make them more confident that they will ultimately be paid back. The original ABF, now referred to as ABF1, has been succeeded by an ABF2, which creates indices and passively managed funds in sovereign and quasi-sovereign bonds denominated in local currencies, its predecessor having been limited to bonds denominated in dollars.

To be sure, there are grounds for questioning the significance and success of these initiatives. In the case of the CMI, the extension of credits beyond the first 20 percent still requires prior negotiation of a program with the IMF. Moreover, its swaps and repos have never actually been activated — not in response to Indonesia's fiscal crisis in the summer of 2005, Thailand's exchange rate and stock market crisis at the end of 2006, or Vietnam's current account crisis in the spring of 2008. East Asian countries are reluctant to point to deficiencies in the policies of their neighbors or to attach demanding conditions to their loans. They are reluctant to infringe on the sovereignty of other nations in a region where political sensitivities often run high. But without firm surveillance and strict conditionality, the CMI will remain a hollow shell. As for the ABMI and ABF1 and 2, Asian bond markets may have grown, but they still lack depth and liquidity. This is especially true of corporate bond markets, the segment that matters most for the development of the Asian economies.

Such reservations notwithstanding, it remains the case that progress has been more extensive in the financial than monetary sphere, where there has been much talk but, as yet, little collective action. The reasons for this difference are not clear. East Asia is highly diverse, both economically and financially, and this heterogeneity of circumstances complicates the task of deciding on a common set of arrangements. But it is not obvious that circumstances relevant to the design of optimal financial arrangements are less heterogeneous than those relevant to choice of monetary-cum-exchange-rate regime. Alternatively, it simply could be that there is more intellectual consensus on the question of how to regulate and develop financial markets than on the appropriate monetary and exchange-rate regime.

Indicative of this wide range of opinions on the question of how to manage exchange rates is the existence of a host of different proposals for enhancing exchange-rate stability. At the less ambitious end of the spectrum are authors like Eichengreen and Ito in this volume who advocate leaving exchange-rate determination to the market but suggest that the volatility of intra-Asian rates will decline to more tolerable levels if central banks adopt inflation targets and pursue them consistently. The question here is not whether inflation targeting in emerging markets is feasible — a growing body of evidence and experience from different regions, including East Asia, confirms that it is. Rather, it is whether coordinated inflation targeting will deliver the requisite exchange-rate stability. Eichengreen cites evidence suggesting that it will, but not everyone may be convinced.

Somewhat more ambitious would be to allow Asian currencies to float subject to some degree of economic management while also taking steps to encourage regional monetary integration. One idea, discussed by Eichengreen *et al.* in this volume, is to create a regional currency — an Asian Currency Unit (ACU) or Regional Currency Unit (RCU) — that would circulate side-by-side with national currencies. Governments would agree on the definition of the RCU as a basket in which the currencies of larger countries have heavier weights. They would issue bonds denominated in RCU. The idea is that international investors would regard RCU-denominated bonds as more attractive than bonds denominated in a single foreign currency, since the diversification offered by a currency basket would offer more stability in terms of domestic purchasing power. Once a market in RCU-denominated sovereign bonds begins to develop, corporations funding themselves internationally may choose to issue RCU-denominated bonds as well. Banks would offer RCU-denominated deposits and extend RCU-denominated loans. In this way, a private market in RCUs would begin to develop. Eventually, trade across borders would be quoted and settled in RCUs. Ultimately, the RCU would come to resemble a regional currency.

This would be a market-led approach to regional monetary integration, consistent with the larger regional integration process in East Asia which is driven more by economics and less by politics than in, inter alia, Europe. The problem is that markets in RCU-denominated assets would be relatively illiquid at the outset. Given the incumbency advantage possessed by existing national currencies, this raises the question of whether the RCU could ever gain significant market share. The case of the European Currency Unit, the internal accounting unit and proto-parallel currency created by the European Community (EC) in 1979, suggests that this is possible but only with concerted efforts by governments. For this approach to succeed, in other words, not just economic but also political leadership will be required after all.

Still more ambitious would be to establish a multilateral exchange-rate grid — an Asian Exchange-Rate System analogous to the European Monetary System (EMS) of the 1980s and 1990s — in which the movement of intra-Asian currencies was limited to narrow fluctuation bands, and governments intervened in the foreign exchange market when the edge of those bands was reached. This option is described by Moon and Rhee in this volume. It is more ambitious than the proposals described above because, given the liquidity of foreign exchange markets, governments and central banks would be committing very extensive resources to such an intervention. It is more ambitious in the sense that they would be subordinating domestic monetary policy to the imperatives of keeping the exchange rate stable. They would be committing to the idea that monetary independence matters less than exchange-rate stability. Finally, this proposal is more ambitious than those described above because the costs of failure would be high. When a central bank commits to pegging the exchange rate but fails, its credibility is damaged. And as the 1997 financial crisis reminds us, the economic and political fallout from such failures can cause serious damage.

The relatively ambitious nature of this approach leads some, such as Eichengreen and De Grauwe in their chapters, to question its feasibility. Governments whose legitimacy rests on their ability to deliver economic growth will not be able to indefinitely subordinate monetary policy to the maintenance of a currency peg. It is not clear who would set the tone for monetary policy systemwide. Asia does not possess a supranational institution analogous to the European Central Bank (ECB) or even an intergovernmental process by which such decisions can be reached collectively. Under such circumstances, monetary conditions presumably would be set by a large country with a strong culture of price stability, which would come to play a role analogous to that of Germany in the EMS. For example, the country in question could be Japan. But a monetary policy that was appropriate for a slowly growing mature economy like Japan might not also be appropriate for a fast-growing developing country like China. The consequent tensions might also excite worries about Japanese dominance. Given the history associated with such fears and tensions, this does not bode well for the durability of such a system. Alternatively, one can imagine China as the country setting the tone for monetary conditions region-wide, given its size and large trade and financial flows with its neighbors. But a China growing a 10 percent a year and battling overheating would presumably prefer much higher interest rates than slower-growing countries like Japan. Moreover, given the volatility of its securities markets, continued weakness of its banks, and unresolved inflation problems, it is not clear that China would be able to assume this leadership role.

And even if all these problems were solved, pegging would still be difficult, given the reality of high capital mobility. Asian central bank reserves may be large, but they are not large enough to buy back the entire money supply, as would be necessary if firms and households sought to liquidate it all at once to avoid the losses resulting from a crisis. A country whose currency fell to the bottom of its fluctuation band would have to receive unlimited support from the system's strong-currency countries. But the latter would be willing to put their own money at risk only if they were confident of being paid back. This would mean attaching strict conditions to their loans. Thus, the viability of a regional exchange-rate system would ultimately run up against the same problems limiting the development of the CMI.

The most ambitious alternative of all would be to move quickly to monetary union, creating an East Asian Central Bank and a single Asian currency. Economically, doing so is straightforward. East Asia today comes as close as Europe in 1999 to satisfying the economic preconditions for smooth operation of a monetary union, as De Grauwe shows in Chapter 6 in this volume. And where preconditions are still absent, they will tend to arise spontaneously in response to the move to a single currency.

Politically, in contrast, an early transition to monetary union would be more challenging. Monetary unification entails a fundamental sacrifice of national monetary sovereignty. Control of national monetary policy is given over to a supranational entity. And national sovereignty is not something that East Asian countries appear willing to sacrifice or pool. At the same time, De Grauwe suggests, again invoking Europe's experience, the political preconditions are as endogenous as their economic equivalents. Take a few steps in the direction of monetary integration — strengthen existing regional mechanisms for policy dialog on monetary policy, for example — and more political willingness will develop. Create an institution responsible for surveillance and advice on East Asian monetary affairs, and out of this seed, he argues, can grow an East Asian Central Bank. Indeed, Chai and Yoon suggest that East Asia already possesses the relevant institution in the form of the CMI and its surveillance mechanism.

Chai and Yoon also offer an interesting twist on the preceding options. Rather than alternatives, they argue, a number of these approaches to monetary integration are in fact complementary and should be pursued simultaneously. In particular, an Asian Monetary System limiting the variability of intra-Asian exchange rates would complement the creation of a RCU. Only if exchange rates were reasonably stable would cross-border trade and financial flows continue to expand strongly, creating a demand for RCU-denominated assets. And only if currency risk was limited to tolerable levels by a credible regional exchange-rate arrangement would investors be willing to hold RCU-denominated bonds. Of course, one can also argue the opposite — that if exchange-rate risk is eliminated there will be a greater willingness on the part of foreign investors to hold bonds denominated in national currencies and a greater tendency to quote and settle trade in domestic units, and therefore no demand for the RCU. This suggests that there is an optimal level of exchange-rate variability, greater than zero but less than infinite, that would optimally complement development of the market in RCUs.

A related point also made by Chai and Moon is that efforts to foster monetary and financial cooperation are strongly complementary. Stable and well-developed financial markets will make it easier for central banks to pursue policies of inflation targeting. In turn, stable exchange-rates, whether achieved through harmonized inflation targeting or a regional exchange-rate mechanism, make it easier to maintain financial stability by reducing the threat from currency mismatches. Stable exchange rates also make it easier to develop deep and liquid bond markets, a fact that has been established in a series of empirical studies.

Regardless of whether the issue is monetary or financial cooperation, progress will heavily depend on the commitment of East Asia's two largest economies, China and Japan. It is revealing in this connection that recent efforts have been spearheaded by ASEAN+3, which expands ASEAN to include China, Japan, and South Korea, and by EMEAP, whose 11 East Asian and Pacific central banks again include China, Japan, and Korea.

The observation is not original to us; the analogy between the role of Germany and France in the European Union (EU) and the role of China and Japan in East Asia has long been noted by aficionados of regional integration. But the final two chapters in the volume, by Yu and Itoh, develop the implications further. Yu describes how China's dynamic growth has brought it to the forefront of international monetary and financial affairs, not just in East Asia but globally. China's exchange rate is a matter of concern for the United States, which sees it as contributing to the problem of global imbalances, but also in other East Asian countries, for which China has emerged as a significant competitor and an important market for final goods. Asian countries may recognize the need to allow their currencies to rise against the dollar and the euro to address the problem of global imbalances, but they hesitate to move until China moves first or unless it moves with them for fear of losing out to Chinese competition.

China, for its part, remains reluctant to let its exchange rate appreciate too rapidly for fear of undermining the operation of a tried-and-true growth model. Industrialists in export-oriented sectors are influential, and the government's legitimacy rests on its ability to deliver export-led growth. China is increasingly aware of its role as a monetary and financial leader, but domestic political and economic constraints continue to limit its ability to exercise that leadership and to promote regional monetary cooperation.

Constraints are also evident in the financial domain. Bank restructuring and financial development are works in progress, as is the development of mechanisms for investing China's international reserves. Yu discusses this last problem, which the Chinese authorities are addressing by creating a sovereign wealth fund. As he explains, the creation of a sovereign wealth fund raises many issues, including those of mandate and administration. There may also be important implications for the other countries of East Asia. These include: will China's sovereign wealth fund invest mainly in the region or elsewhere, and will it act as a buy-and-hold investor or trade actively and thus add liquidity to regional financial markets?

Itoh, in the closing Chapter 8, argues that Japan has long been conscious of its stake in East Asia and that it has sought to exercise monetary and financial leadership. An example is its proposal in 1997 to create an Asian Monetary Fund, an initiative that foundered on opposition from the IMF and the United States and received a lukewarm reception in China. As this episode illustrated, Japan's leadership efforts must overcome the legacies of history: other East Asian countries, still mindful of Japanese expansionism in the first half of the 20th century, worry that Japanese leadership would mean Japanese control. In addition, Japan, like China, faces political constraints on its ability to lead and even support regional cooperation. Itoh cites the example of Japanese farmers, whose opposition has hindered efforts to negotiate regional trade agreements. At the same time, he suggests that the situation is changing and that domestic politics may pose less of an obstacle in the future than the past.

The end result of these processes is clear: East Asia will become more integrated both monetarily and financially. The question is exactly how and when. It is our hope that this volume takes us some way toward answering it.

CHAPTER 2

Fostering Monetary and Exchange-Rate Cooperation in East Asia

Barry Eichengreen

Introduction

Leaders in East Asia are consistent in calling for cooperation to stabilize exchange rates.[1] Their call is heard in periods of slow growth and periods of rapid growth. It is advanced when the yen is weak and when the yen is strong. Though heard prior to the financial crisis of 1997–98, their case gained additional adherents as a result of that episode and its repercussions. And the argument for the cooperative management of exchange rates continues to be advanced despite the persistent skepticism outside the region.

One cannot help but be reminded of the importance that European officials attached to exchange-rate stability in the second half of the 20th century.[2] Efforts to deepen monetary cooperation in order to facilitate the transition to a single currency were evident in Europe already in the 1950s.[3] They were rooted in memories of a financial crisis in the 1930s

---

[1] In this chapter, I sometimes refer to Asia rather than East Asia for ease of exposition. In either case, I should be understood to mean the ASEAN+3 countries (ASEAN plus China, South Korea, and Japan). In some contexts, that of the Chiang Mai Initiative (CMI), for example, it may make sense to also include Australia and New Zealand under the big tent.

[2] Not least in the skepticism with which outside observers similarly viewed Europe's integrationist initiatives (recall how many non-European economists doubted that the euro would ever be created).

[3] The issue had already been raised by American Marshall Plan administrators in the second half of the 1940s. It was then kept alive by Paul-Henri Spaak in discussions of the Treaty of Rome, by Robert Marjolin and Pierre Uri in the agencies of the European Economic Community, by Robert Triffin in the halls of academia, and by Jean Monnet through his Action Committee for the United States of Europe.

that had destabilized currencies, fanning economic, and political tensions; European leaders concluded that stabilizing exchange rates was essential for preventing the recurrence of similarly destructive events. Support was fostered by the growth of intra-regional trade as Europe's economies recovered from World War II and then by successive trade agreements, starting with the Common Market of the Six. The movement was lent impetus by the instability of the dollar, previously the anchor for the region's currencies, following the breakdown of Bretton Woods. The result was a series of initiatives to promote exchange-rate stability and an eventual transition to monetary union: the Werner Report, the Snake, the Snake in the Tunnel, the European Monetary System (EMS), and finally the euro. It is not hard to see analogous factors in the push for monetary and exchange-rate coordination in Asia, from memories of financial crisis to the growth of intra-regional trade and the instability of the dollar. And it is not surprising in this light that more than a few observers have suggested emulating Europe's example.

But one should not ignore respects in which Asia is different. Financial markets are substantially deregulated and open to international capital flows, something that was not the case in Europe as late as the 1980s. Stabilizing currencies is more difficult in this environment of high capital mobility. In addition, there is not the same degree of political solidarity as prevailed in Europe. There is a greater reluctance to pool sovereignty, in turn making it more difficult to create transnational institutions of monetary governance akin to the European Central Bank. And where European monetary integration took place in a world in which pegging was the norm, countries today are moving away from exchange-rate-centered monetary policy strategies. This reflects an alternative framework — inflation targeting — that did not yet exist in this earlier period. It reflects the existence of financial markets and instruments with which exchange risk can be hedged, easing life with flexible rates. Whatever the explanation, exchange-rate stability and monetary stability are not regarded as synonymous to the same extent as in Western Europe in the second half of the 20th century.

These differences suggest that efforts to foster monetary and exchange-rate cooperation will have to proceed differently in Asia. They must accommodate the reality of capital mobility. They will have to acknowledge the existence of different political constraints. And they should capitalize on the existence of new approaches to the conduct of monetary policy.

These observations provide points of departure for thinking about three approaches to encouraging monetary cooperation in the region: exchange-rate pegging, a parallel regional currency, and harmonized inflation targeting. In what follows, I describe these options and evaluate them relative to the three aforementioned criteria: robustness with respect to capital mobility, compatibility with prevailing political circumstances, and congruence with modern ideas about the conduct of monetary policy.

I find the exchange-rate-centered option problematic on all three grounds. While the parallel currency approach has more appeal, it is unlikely to provide the desired level of stability over what could be a very long transition to a regional currency. Harmonized inflation targeting is the best option for delivering monetary and exchange-rate stability and laying the groundwork for monetary integration while respecting the prevailing financial, political, and technical constraints.

Exchange-Rate-Centered Options

The East Asian miracle has long been associated with stable, competitively valued currencies. The yen was pegged at 360 to the dollar for more than two decades, coincident with Japan's high-growth era. More recently, the renminbi has been linked to the dollar, a policy that has helped to sustain China's remarkable economic growth. These are only two prominent examples of a general phenomenon. East Asian economic growth has been export led, and a stable and competitively valued exchange rate has been integral to that process. The result is a tendency, understandable in the circumstances, to associate exchange-rate stability with economic growth and to view the former as a prerequisite for the latter.

Traditionally, stability meant stability against the dollar. Recently, however, this association has grown problematic. With the dollar fluctuating against other major currencies, stability vis-à-vis the dollar no longer guarantees stability vis-à-vis East Asia's leading extra-regional markets. With the growth of capital mobility, stabilizing against the dollar means that regional monetary conditions are set in Washington, DC, even though the policies that the Federal Reserve deems appropriate for the United States may not be suitable to the very different circumstances of Asia. With the growth of the US current account deficit, the failure of currencies like the renminbi to adjust more rapidly against the dollar raises the specter of protectionism in the US Congress. The prospect of a decline in the effective exchange rate of the dollar as part of the adjustment needed to narrow the US current account deficit points up these dangers. It augurs instability vis-à-vis other currencies like the euro. It raises risks of inflation and overheating as Asian exports are rendered more and more competitive on international markets. It invites a protectionist backlash in the United States.

The obvious alternative is pegging to a basket. There has been no shortage of proposals for doing so.[4] And, not surprisingly, some Asian economies have been moving in this direction.[5] Basket pegging links East Asian monetary conditions to the state of the world economy rather than just to economic conditions in the United States. It leaves scope for adjustment against the dollar to help correct global imbalances and defuse trade tensions without undermining export competitiveness. Acknowledging the fact that vertically specialized intra-regional trade is the most rapidly expanding component of East Asian exports, it is possible to include Asian currencies as well as extra-Asian currencies in the basket, thereby stabilizing effective rates, something that countries like Singapore and, more recently, China have done. The logical culmination of this train of thought is for each regional currency to be pegged to other regional currencies, creating a multilateral currency grid like the EMS and ensuring exchange-rate stability within the region.[6] Monetarily, this would make East Asia more like the Euro area or the United States — that is, a large economically integrated zone within which exchange-rate volatility has been eliminated and which, by virtue of its size, can regard fluctuations vis-à-vis the rest of the world with an attitude of benign neglect.

But pegs, including basket pegs, have drawbacks in terms of their robustness with respect to capital mobility, their compatibility with prevailing political circumstances, and their congruence with state-of-the-art monetary policy strategies. Pegs are difficult to defend in an environment of high capital mobility. They require monetary conditions to be strictly

---

[4] To name, but a few, see Kawai (2005), Williamson (2005), and Yoshitomi (2007).

[5] Thus, Kawai (2007a) estimates Frankel-Wei regressions designed to recover the weights on the major currencies in different countries' implicit currency baskets and finds some tendency for the weight on the dollar to fall, and weights on other currencies to rise, over time.

[6] Choi (2007) describes how a basket dominated by extra-regional currencies could give way over time to a basket based on Asian currencies.

harmonized with those in the rest of the world. To be sure, all currency pegs operate as narrow bands or exchange-rate target zones, reflecting the existence of transactions costs. They specify not just the central parity but also ceilings and floors within which the rate can fluctuate.[7] This leaves some scope for domestic monetary autonomy.[8] But such autonomy is limited and, in any case, exists only if the band is credible, which constrains not just current but also prospective future policy. Defending a peg when the markets are free to bet against you requires the authorities to subordinate other goals to the overriding imperative of stabilizing the exchange rate. And this is not something to which governments in democratic societies, where citizens prioritize goals such as employment and growth, can credibly commit.[9]

At the same time, abandoning a peg, thereby controverting a whole series of earlier statements reiterating the commitment to the regime, can tarnish the credibility of the authorities and threaten their political livelihood.[10] This creates a tendency to attempt to defend the indefensible. When the crisis then comes, the consequences can be severe. The experience of the Asian crisis drove home these observations: the difficulty of exiting a regime or even just a specific peg when no longer appropriate, the costs of unsuitable monetary conditions, and the impossibility of defending the status quo when the markets turn. Similarly, Europe's experience with these problems, culminating in the EMS crisis of 1992–93, motivated the decision to abandon currency pegs by moving to the euro in 1999. In a sense it was the removal of capital controls, consequent on the decision in 1986 to create a single market in goods and factor services (including capital), that forced the issue, precipitating the crisis, the abandonment of EMS pegs, and the transition to the euro.[11] There is no more immediate example of the fragility of EMS-type arrangements in the face of high capital mobility.

---

[7] See Giovaninni (1989) for a discussion of this point in connection with the gold standard, Bretton Woods, and the EMS.

[8] This is the lesson of the literature on exchange-rate target zones; see Krugman (1991).

[9] This is the central message of Eichengreen (1996). From this point of view, it is not surprising that less than fully democratic regimes, including that historically of Hong Kong, have had the greatest success in maintaining currency pegs.

[10] The idea that devaluing or abandoning a peg has serious costs goes back to Cooper (1971), whose empirical work was updated by Frankel (2005).

[11] And, in the case of the minority of European Union (EU) member states unprepared to sign on to the single currency (Sweden and the United Kingdom), to the abandonment of pegs in favor of more freely floating exchange rates backed by inflation targeting.

Political solidarity sufficient to lend credibility to the commitment of strong-currency countries to support their weak-currency counterparts when their common regional arrangement comes under attack can, in principle, finesse this dilemma. This brings us to the second evaluation criterion, namely, the compatibility of arrangements with prevailing political circumstances and constraints. In EMS-style arrangements where regional currencies are yoked together in a multilateral currency grid, the weakness of one currency automatically translates into the strength of others. That is, if one regional currency falls against the basket, others must rise against the basket as a matter of definition. Countries in a strong position can then use their own currency to purchase that of the issuer in distress, in effect making a loan to the regional partner. To the extent that shocks are asymmetrically distributed across countries, the same conclusion applies when exchange rates are pegged to an extra-regional currency or currencies. Countries in a relatively strong position will then be able to lend reserves to neighbors in a position of weakness. And since the East Asian central banks and governments possess such ample reserves, there should be no difficulty in facing down the markets.

The problem is that, absent guarantees, governments and central banks are not prepared to provide large amounts of reserves or even purchase large amounts of the problem country's currency. They will want assurances that they will be repaid and that the problems requiring them to intervene will not recur. Governments therefore attach conditions to their loans. They monitor whether corrective measures are being taken. They are not willing to provide unlimited resources, in contrast to international financial markets, which are able to mobilize essentially unlimited amounts of liquidity to attack a currency. In Europe, the EMS Articles of Agreement obliged strong-currency countries to provide unlimited support to their weak-currency counterparts through the short-term and very short-term financing facilities. But Germany, which anticipated that it would regularly find itself to be the strong-currency country, obtained an opt-out, which it implicitly invoked in 1992.[12] Even though France and

---

[12] Specifically, Otmar Emminger, the head of the German Bundesbank, obtained a statement of reassurance from his government, the so-called "Emminger letter," authorizing the Bundesbank to opt out in the event that its commitment to price stability was threatened. As Otto Graf Lambsdorff, the German Economics Minister, made clear in a speech to the Bundestag at the end of 1978, the commitment to unlimited intervention would always be subordinate to the Bundesbank Act of 1957 giving the German central bank a mandate to pursue price stability. See Eichengreen (2007a), Chapter 8.

Germany were committed to building an "ever closer Europe," in the memorable words of the Treaty of Rome, such a political solidarity as existed did not translate into a willingness to extend unlimited support.

East Asia's equivalent of the short-term and very-short-term financing facilities is the CMI of currency swaps and credits. Although its goals remain constructively ambiguous, one can imagine that the reserves committed to the CMI could be used to support currencies experiencing pressure. The CMI has been expanded repeatedly.[13] Most recently, participating countries have committed to multilateralizing it (transforming the earmarked resources from bilateral credit lines into a common reserve pool).[14] But there is a reluctance to actually extend credits: the CMI was activated neither when the interaction of high energy prices with fuel subsidies undermined confidence in the Indonesian rupiah in 2005 nor when the awkward imposition of capital controls disturbed Thai markets in 2006.[15] Political relations between lending and borrowing countries are more distant than that in Europe. The lenders are not in a position to apply firm surveillance and demand difficult adjustments by the borrowers. Worried about whether they will be paid back, they therefore hesitate to lend. The need to strengthen multilateral surveillance is well known, but this desire runs up against the reluctance of Asian countries to openly criticize their neighbors.[16] Political realities thus constitute a second reason for skepticism about the durability of a multilateral currency grid.

Nor does an exchange-rate peg represent state-of-the-art monetary policy. Pegging outsources the commitment to low inflation to the central bank issuing the currency to which the exchange rate is pegged. But outsourcing can be less credible than producing the commitment to price stability at home. Limited credibility also limits resort to the escape clause if it becomes necessary to adjust policy in response to, say, a slowdown

---

[13] At the time of writing, agreement has been reached on some $80 billion of bilateral swap agreements among the ASEAN+3 countries. Kawai (2007b), p. 17.

[14] Discussions of multilateralizing the CMI took place on the sidelines of the spring 2007 meetings of the Asian Development Bank (ADB) (see China Economic Net, 2007).

[15] In addition, the CMI has had no evident effect in slowing the rate of growth of reserves in the countries on the receiving end of its bilateral swaps. If the CMI really represented a credible reserve-sharing arrangement, one would expect self-insurance through reserve accumulation to slow down. The fact that it has not sheds some light on the commitment to co-insure.

[16] See Manzano (2001), Manupipatpong (2002), and De Brouwer and Wang (2003).

in growth. Here flexible inflation targeting, described in more detail in the Section "Harmonized Inflation Targeting" below, may offer a superior solution. Some countries (Israel for example) attempted to combine an exchange-rate rule with an inflation target but moved away from this hybrid arrangement after experiencing conflicts between the two goals.[17]

Thus, the exchange-rate-centered approach to monetary cooperation fails to satisfy the three criteria set out above: robustness with respect to capital mobility, compatibility with prevailing political circumstances and constraints, and congruence with state-of-the-art monetary policy strategies.

A Parallel Currency

An alternative approach to monetary cooperation is to create a parallel regional currency.[18] This idea has been pushed by the ADB and its president, Haruhiko Kuroda. As described by Kuroda (2006), the Asian Currency Unit (ACU), defined as a weighted average of the 13 ASEAN+3 currencies, might start as a convenient summary indicator of the strength of Asian currencies vis-à-vis those of the rest of the world. But it also could be a convenient unit in which to denominate bonds for Asian investors seeking currency diversification and for issuers wishing to hedge the currency risk of receivables denominated in regional currencies. The ADB and other official institutions could jump-start the market in the instrument by issuing their own ACU-denominated bonds.

Allowing an ACU to circulate alongside national currencies would have three advantages. First, it would not be necessary to stabilize exchange rates between the currencies comprising the basket; hence, fragility would be less. Second, the parallel currency would be more stable than any one national currency in terms of aggregate Asian production and exports; it would thus be a vehicle for encouraging intra-regional trade and investment. Third, the decision to move to a single currency could be driven by economics rather than politics. Only when a critical mass of producers, exporters, and investors had adopted the parallel

---

[17] For discussion, see Leiderman and Bar-Or (2002).
[18] This section draws liberally on Eichengreen (2006). See also Mori *et al.* (2002) and Aggarwala (2003).

currency would it be clear that Asian economies were ready for monetary unification.

The ACU could be defined as a fixed number of units of each constituent currency. While the quantity of each component currency would remain fixed, its contribution to the value of the ACU would vary with its exchange rate; as currencies depreciated, their weight in the ACU would decline. The composition of the basket might be revised periodically to reflect the changing weights of the participating countries. Weights could be determined by the share of the country in regional GDP or exports.

Official ACUs would be created in exchange for swaps of a fraction of the international reserves of participating central banks. The amount of these swaps could change periodically to reflect changes in the quantity and value of those gold and dollar reserves. Participating central banks would agree to accept ACUs in transactions among themselves.

The existence of these benchmarks would make it more attractive for both financial and non-financial firms to issue and accept ACU-denominated liabilities and assets, subject to standard prudential regulations. Bond or deposit documentation would specify that when the composition of the official ACU basket changed, the value of private ACU assets and liabilities would change accordingly. The value of the private ACU would be guaranteed by the commitment of the issuer (such as a bank accepting a deposit) to convert the instrument into its underlying components. Arbitrage would prevent significant divergences from opening up between the value of the private ACU and the constituent currencies.

This approach resembles another European precedent: efforts to use the ECU as a stepping-stone to monetary unification. The ECU was defined in 1974 as a basket of currencies of the members of the European Community (EC) for purposes of EC accounting. It was adopted in 1975 as the unit of account for the European Development Fund and then for the European Investment Bank and the EC budget. With the establishment of the EMS in 1979, participating countries were supposed to stabilize their exchange rates against the ECU basket. Currency positions acquired as the result of interventions were similarly to be settled in ECU.

But the ECU never acquired a significant role in the business of the EC and in the EMS in particular. Although credits within the EMS were denominated in ECU, they were extended in national currencies. Rather than actually basing EMS parities on an ECU central rate, that central rate was only used to compute bilateral rates, which became the focus for central banks and the markets. The ECU's unit of account role was limited to the financial accounts of EC institutions and a few European corporations engaging in extensive cross-border business. In the 1990s, only about 1 percent of trade within the Community was invoiced in ECUs. At their height, ECU-denominated claims still amounted to less than 10 percent of the non-dollar foreign currency claims of banks reporting to the Bank for International Settlements. European Currency Unit bonds never accounted for much more than 20 percent of all non-dollar Eurobonds. Medium-term ECU notes accounted for barely 15 percent of the non-US dollar market in such notes, European Currency Unit commercial paper accounted for only about 10 percent of all euro-commercial paper.

The question is why. One answer is that it was unattractive to move to the ECU in the absence of evidence that others were prepared to do likewise. It was unattractive for individual European producers to set prices in ECU unless other European producers did so, limiting transactions costs. It was unattractive for individual financial institutions to float bonds denominated in ECU unless other financial institutions did likewise, creating the critical mass needed for the creation of a deep and liquid secondary market. It was unattractive to quote product prices in ECU so long as wages and other domestically sourced inputs were priced in the national currency. Money is characterized by network externalities; it pays to use the same medium of exchange and unit of account as other market participants.[19] As with any other network, there is a tendency for the status quo to be locked in. Governments can attempt to make the parallel currency more attractive by giving it legal tender status alongside the national currency. But the incentive to continue relying on the national currency will remain strong. Efforts to promote the use of the parallel currency may have to overcome considerable inertia.

By design, this parallel-currency scheme is intended to encourage banks, firms, and households to take on ACU-denominated claims. But if some end up with more ACU liabilities than assets, they will then be subject to currency-mismatch problems and heightened financial fragility. If banks match their ACU liabilities and loans, then the currency risk will simply be transferred to their corporate customers, saddling the banking

---

[19] See Dowd and Greenaway (1993).

system with heightened credit risk. Liquidity risk can also result if depositors are aware of these vulnerabilities and run on the banking system. These risks can be contained by tightening prudential supervision and regulation to ensure that banks hold sufficient liquid ACU assets and constituent foreign currency assets to avert a run. The central bank should hold additional foreign reserves in ACU or constituent foreign currencies in order to be able to replenish the ACU reserves of the banking system. The authorities should consider a managed float to encourage banks and firms to hedge their ACU exposures.

But forcing banks and governments to hold additional foreign currency reserves would have a significant opportunity cost. Limiting their ability to incur liabilities in ACU would prevent them from issuing additional ACU-denominated bonds and thereby enhancing the liquidity of secondary markets. Forcing banks to hold additional foreign currency reserves would limit the growth of intermediation. And, given the gap between the promulgation and enforcement of prudential regulations, it is not clear that tighter supervision would ultimately succeed in containing the risk to stability. The conclusion of much of the literature is that partially dollarized economies should move forward to full dollarization or back toward a predominantly domestic currency basis.[20] This suggests that an extended period when the parallel currency circulates alongside national currencies could be one of heightened financial fragility.

Moreover, limiting the freedom of banks to accept ACU deposits in excess of their ability to make ACU loans and otherwise restraining the growth of transactions in ACU claims would slow the spread of the parallel currency. Inevitably, then, the parallel-currency route to monetary integration could be a lengthy one.

To gain widespread acceptance, the ACU will have to out-compete not just existing Asian currencies but also the dollar, which is widely used for cross-border transactions in the region, as noted above. This observation has led authors like Robert Mundell to advocate that Asian countries should adopt the dollar as a "common parallel currency" — that is, as an officially recognized currency for use in invoicing and settling trade.[21] But, as intra-Asian trade continues to grow, invoicing and settling in a common Asian currency will become more attractive relative to invoicing and settling in dollars. In any case, Asian countries are reluctant to give

---

[20] See for example Di Nicolo *et al.* (2003).
[21] The language is from Mundell (2002).

the currency of an outside power legal tender status for domestic transactions. As a result, the residents of an Asian country must still convert dollars into the national currency when making tax payments or engaging in other domestic transactions requiring a unit with legal tender status. Under the parallel-currency approach, Asian governments would give the ACU full legal tender status for domestic use, which would make it more attractive. There are also reasons to think that the dollar will grow more volatile relative to Asian currencies as Asian countries relax and abandon their pegs to the greenback in the interest of greater flexibility and to the extent that America's twin deficits lead to a weaker dollar. This will make using ACUs, rather than dollars, more attractive. Finally, the hold of network externalities and therefore the advantages of incumbency may be less in our financially sophisticated age than was the case in the past. Given the proliferation of instruments in financial markets and the decline in bid-ask spreads, it is easier for market participants to contemplate alternatives.

How does the parallel-currency approach stack up against our three criteria for a viable approach to monetary cooperation and integration? It is congruent with political conditions and constraints: it does not require significant sovereign prerogatives to be delegated to a transnational entity; in particular, national central banks retain control over their monetary policies so long as the national currency has significant market share. The approach is consistent with the image of integration as being driven more by economics and less than politics in Asia than in Europe. It is compatible with financial deregulation and capital mobility. Indeed, it capitalizes on their existence by encouraging the creation of new financial instruments and encouraging their circulation internationally. In particular, the greater is cross-border bond issuance and investment in the region, the more attractive it should be to denominate such issues in the parallel currency. Finally, the parallel-currency approach is compatible with state-of-the-art monetary policy practices insofar as national central banks can continue to pursue inflation targeting so long as there remains a demand for the national currency. Inflation control may be more complex if there are unpredictable shifts between individual national currencies and the parallel composite currency, but historical experience neither suggests that the circulation of a parallel currency makes inflation forecasting and inflation control impossible nor does the literature on partially dollarized banking systems suggest that these jeopardize price stability.[22] The parallel currency is likely to gain market share only slowly. The inertia favoring national currencies is strong. Prudential policies limiting the risks to financial stability created by currency mismatches will also slow adoption of the parallel currency. But if this means that the process culminating in a single Asian currency takes time to unfold, this is not necessarily a bad thing, especially since years will have to pass before the entire range of supportive conditions is in place for Asian monetary unification.

Harmonized Inflation Targeting

A third option for monetary cooperation is harmonized inflation targeting. At the national level, this means substituting an inflation target for an exchange-rate target as the anchor for monetary policy. The full framework entails not just empowering the central bank to set an inflation target but also requiring it to release an inflation forecast and to explain how it will deliver an outcome consistent with that forecast, as well as to publish an inflation report explaining deviations between forecasts and realizations.[23] The appeal of inflation targeting is that policy credibility is grown at home. Policy can be tailored to domestic price-level pressures instead of simply hoping that foreign monetary conditions are suitable for domestic circumstances.[24] As the central bank gains credibility, it can allow deviations from target inflation in the short run as necessary to damp short-run output and employment fluctuations.[25] If the medium-term

---

[22] See Reinhart *et al.* (2003).

[23] For an introduction to inflation targeting experience, see Bernanke *et al.* (1999) and Mishkin and Schmidt-Hebbel (2001). As typically formulated, the full inflation targeting framework entails public announcement of medium-term inflation targets, an institutional commitment to price stability, an information-inclusive approach to setting policy instruments, a transparent monetary policy strategy, and an increased accountability of the central bank for attaining its inflation objectives.

[24] As will have to be the case if foreign monetary conditions are imported via the currency peg.

[25] This is known as flexible inflation targeting.

inflation target is fully credible, then loosening credit in the short run in order to support output and employment will do little to fan inflation. This balance between credibility and flexibility has led a growing number of countries, including Asian countries, to adopt this framework.[26]

Note that the exchange-rate plays a subsidiary role when monetary policy is conducted in this fashion. The central bank commits to hitting an inflation target, not an exchange-rate target. When these two conflict, it is the exchange rate that has to give in.[27] If a country retains capital controls, then there may be some scope for pursuing separate inflation and exchange-rate targets, as in China today. But that scope is limited when capital markets are open, as is increasingly the case.[28] If the central bank loosens in order to prevent the exchange rate from appreciating, for example, then inflation will overshoot, undermining the credibility of policy regime. If the central bank is truly committed to targeting inflation, then targeting the exchange rate will have to be sacrificed.

This is not to say that the exchange rate plays no role in open-economy inflation targeting. The exchange rate can be one of the most important variables for forecasting inflation in an open economy, and the central bank will want to pay it close attention. But this is not because the authorities care about the exchange rate per se; it is because the exchange rate helps them anticipate movements in the variable that they do care about, namely, inflation.[29]

Harmonized inflation targeting would entail a group of countries agreeing on inflation targets. If chosen appropriately, that agreement might also have the ancillary benefit of limiting exchange-rate instability. Assume, for the sake of exposition, that relative purchasing-power-parity holds — that the domestic inflation rate minus the foreign inflation rate equals the rate of depreciation of the currency. By implementing targets for inflation, two countries can then determine the rate of change of their

---

[26] Rose (2006) provides a list of countries that have adopted this regime.

[27] Recall that this was the experience, as noted above, of early inflation targeters such as Israel that attempted to pursue both inflation and exchange-rate targets simultaneously.

[28] And which will presumably be even more the case in the future.

[29] The particulars vary depending on the structure of the economy — whether the exchange rate is driven by foreign or domestic shocks, whether the foreign exchange market is dominated by current or capital account transactions, and whether or not exchange-rate movements have important balance sheet effects with implications for the credit channel and financial stability. But the general point remains the same. See Eichengreen (2007b).

bilateral exchange rate. If they agree on common inflation targets, the exchange rate will be stable under the assumption of relative PPP.[30]

In practice, something resembling PPP, whether relative or absolute, holds only in the medium to long run; exchange rates deviate from the level predicted by that relationship in the short run. But it can still be argued that the exchange rate will be more stable when two countries target inflation than when they do not.[31] A credible policy of inflation targeting provides an anchor for expectations, and the existence of that anchor will help to stabilize foreign exchange markets. Investors will no longer have reason to believe that high inflation today is a leading indicator of high inflation tomorrow, since the authorities have now committed to low inflation. They will pay a political price if they miss their target, and they will have to provide an explanation for any failure. Each bit of inflationary news will not cause the exchange rate to jump, because investors have reason to doubt that inflationary news today augers further inflation tomorrow. Speculation in the foreign exchange market will become stabilizing rather than destabilizing. Exchange rates will settle down.

There is an empirical support for this view. Kuttner and Posen (2001) use data for 41 developing countries, relating exchange-rate volatility to whether or not a country targets inflation (and to measures of central bank autonomy and the declared exchange-rate regime). They find that exchange-rate volatility is less in inflation targeters, although the effect is not statistically significant at conventional confidence levels. Using data for 45 developing and advanced countries, Rose (2006) also finds that inflation targeters have significantly lower exchange-rate volatility than other countries.

Eichengreen and Taylor (2004) have also looked at the determinants of bilateral exchange-rate volatility in a multicountry model. They model

---

[30] A complication is that relative PPP is even remotely plausible only for the prices of traded goods, whereas inflation targets are set in terms of consumer prices (or consumer prices net of volatile energy- and commodity-related components). Because non-traded goods have a weight in the consumer price index and rise faster in fast-growing low-income economies (due to the operation of the Balassa-Samuelson effect), keeping the exchange rate stable may require low-income countries to maintain a somewhat higher inflation target.

[31] The locus classicus of this argument is Eichengreen and Taylor (2004), on which the following text and argument build.

bilateral exchange-rate volatility as a function of a vector of economic and financial characteristics in each country pair, and in addition of whether one or both central banks are inflation targeters. Because the decision to target inflation may be endogenous, they instrument this variable using the M2/GDP ratio (on the grounds that countries with deeper financial markets find it easier to target inflation) and with a measure of transparency and corruption from *Transparency International* (on the grounds that inflation targeting is easier in countries where transparency is part of the economic and political culture). They find that exchange-rate volatility is less when one or both countries target inflation. This appears to be the case whether or not instruments are used for inflation targeting and whether or not a separate measure of the exchange-rate regime is included.

The results thus suggest that inflation targeting may go some way toward limiting exchange-rate volatility. They also suggest that this regime is likely to be more durable and less crisis-prone than exchange-rate targeting, in that no country adopting inflation targeting has, so far, abandoned that regime either voluntarily or under duress. This means that exchange-rate volatility can actually be less in the medium term in countries that target inflation than in countries that seek to peg the exchange rate (and ultimately fail).[32]

Inflation targeting presupposes the absence of fiscal dominance (that monetary policy is not subordinated to chronic budget deficits). It assumes financial development sufficient to establish a reliable link between the central bank's instruments and inflation outcomes. More generally, it assumes the ability to reliably forecast inflation. Not all of these conditions may be present in developing countries. But reservations regarding inflation targeting in developing countries have receded as more such countries have adopted the regime (inter alia Indonesia, Turkey, and Peru). For inflation targeting to anchor expectations, it is not necessary to adopt the entire framework at the outset; Peru, for example, adopted an inflation target without releasing forecasts, publishing an inflation report, etc. (It has since begun doing so.) Thus, early warnings that inflation targeting is too demanding for developing countries may have been overdrawn.

Still, there is reason to question the feasibility of inflation targeting in the low-income members of ASEAN (Cambodia, Laos, Myanmar, and

---

[32] Something also pointed out by Rose (2006).

Vietnam), given the underdevelopment of their financial systems, the absence of a culture of transparency, and central banks' lack of operational independence. But these countries have an alternative, namely pegged exchange rates, because they retain capital controls (as a corollary of that same financial underdevelopment). This is a reminder that one-size-fits-all advice is not likely to provide a path to monetary and exchange-rate cooperation in East Asia.

How does harmonized inflation targeting rate in terms of our three evaluation criteria? The regime is robust relative to financial liberalization and capital mobility, in that it avoids creating fixed prices against which speculators can bet. As Rose (2006) notes, inflation targeters experience a low incidence of sudden stops in capital flows, and no inflation targeter has yet experienced a full-fledged banking crisis. Inflation targeting is congruent with modern principles of monetary policy in that it encourages central bank independence and accountability, a commitment to price stability, and the use of an information-inclusive operating strategy. And it is consistent with Asia's political circumstances in that it does not assume a degree of political solidarity — and therefore a willingness to compromise national sovereignty — that does not exist.

Conclusion

The desire for exchange-rate stability in East Asia is strong. It is rooted in the association of stable exchange rates with the economic miracle. It is buttressed by memories of the 1997–98 financial crisis, when currency volatility precipitated balance-sheet problems and financial distress. It is reinforced by the expansion of vertically organized intra-regional trade and the emergence of China as a low-cost assembly platform. It appeals to those who see exchange-rate stabilization as a stepping-stone to the monetary union.

Yet, a regional exchange-rate arrangement analogous to the EMS of the 1980s and 1990s also has drawbacks. History shows that pegged-rate regimes are short-lived. They are especially short-lived when financial systems are deregulated and capital accounts are open. And the costs of their collapse can be considerable, something that Asian observers should appreciate given their own experience a decade ago. They require a high level of political solidarity — a willingness to create transnational institutions of monetary governance and to delegate policy to those institutions.

East Asian countries might be prepared to pool their monetary sovereignty in this way sometime in the future. But that date is still distant. In the meantime, exchange-rate pegging remains risky business. While cooperation in pegging exchange rates can be a logical step on the path to deeper monetary integration, it can also be a misstep if things go wrong.

Two alternatives that go some way toward meeting the desire for stable exchange rates, while consensus on the desirability of an Asian monetary union is still being forged, are a parallel currency and harmonized inflation targeting. A parallel regional currency provides a stable unit for intra-regional trade and investment. Inflation targeting limits exchange-rate volatility, in turn limiting the need for expensive hedging transactions. Both approaches are thus capable of lending further impetus to the growth of intra-regional trade and investment.

But the parallel-currency approach is unproven. There are few historical examples of synthetic, basket-based parallel currencies that have gained significant market share. And the fact that the market in the parallel currency will start out small and that liquidity will be limited will mean significant transactions costs for those using it in intra-regional trade and investment. Inflation targeting, in contrast, is a proven strategy. Central banks in East Asia and elsewhere have accumulated considerable experience with its operation. Its corresponding drawback is that it will only reduce exchange-rate volatility, not eliminate it. It therefore will not lend the same impetus to the expansion of intra-regional trade and investment as a hypothetical arrangement where exchange risk is removed.

The choice is thus between a risky strategy that not only promises to eliminate exchange risk in the short-run but also heightens the danger of running off the rails, and a pair of safer strategies that not only reduce exchange risk but are likely to prove more robust and durable. Given the experience of 1997–98, East Asian policy makers have good reasons to opt for the latter.

CHAPTER 3

The Connections Between Financial and Monetary Cooperation in East Asia[1]

Hee-Yul Chai and Deok Ryong Yoon

Introduction

One of the most important achievements in regional financial cooperation since the Asian crisis of 1997–98 was the creation of the Chiang Mai Initiative (CMI) by the ASEAN+3 countries in 2000. The objective of the CMI is the preservation of financial stability. At its center is a network of bilateral swap arrangements among the participating countries. More recently, ASEAN+3 finance ministers organized a task force to study the multilateralization of the CMI with the goal of creating what we will call in this chapter the "Post-CMI."[2]

Another step in the direction of financial cooperation is the Asian Bond Market Initiative (ABMI). The ABMI was proposed at a meeting of ASEAN+3 deputy finance ministers in 2002. It is designed to enhance the access of emerging Asian countries to bond finance by reducing the risks of cross-border investment. Six working groups have been studying these issues under the umbrella of the AMBI.[3]

Monetary cooperation has not received commensurate attention. By monetary cooperation, we mean collaborative efforts to foster intra-regional exchange-rate stability and/or exchange-rate stability vis-à-vis a third currency like the US dollar. Initiatives directed toward increasing the

---

[1] We are grateful to Barry Eichengreen, Masahisro Kawai, Woosik Moon, and Yeongseop Rhee for their helpful comments.

[2] The 10th ASEAN+3 Finance Ministers' Meeting (AFMM) held in Kyoto in May 2007 made public a broad outline of the Post-CMI.

[3] The technical issues, in particular, turned out to be more difficult than previously envisioned and, as a result, the ABMI's progress is still slow.

international use of Asian currencies and creating a regional currency also fall under this heading. There have been a variety of proposals for monetary cooperation, primarily within academic circles, and the finance ministers of three Northeast Asian countries — South Korea, China, and Japan — have reaffirmed their commitment to the introduction of a regional current unit (RCU).[4] While the shape and functions of the RCU are still to be determined, this statement of finance ministers is a concrete step in the direction of more systematic monetary cooperation.

Monetary and financial cooperation may be analytically distinct, but initiatives in either area will have implications for the other. We focus on the implications of the introduction of the RCU for the Post-CMI and the ABMI. We show, for example, that use of the RCU will enable the Post-CMI to more effectively pursue its goal of buttressing financial stability and enhancing intra-regional exchange-rate stability. Similarly, the development of bond markets will be easier if the RCU is actively used in the region as a means of payment, unit of account, and currency of denomination for financial assets. But for the RCU to come into widespread use, market forces will have to be supplemented by public policy measures, which will in turn require meaningful political commitment. This is a challenging agenda for Asian policymakers.

These observations also have implications for the prospects for regional monetary integration. If markets in RCU-denominated assets develop successfully, then the RCU will provide further impetus for monetary integration. Specifically, if the RCU develops into an actively used parallel currency, it could serve as a vehicle for the parallel-currency approach to monetary unification described by Eichengreen in Chapter 2 of this volume. On the other hand, if Asian policymakers fail to foster widespread use of the RCU, this route to regional monetary integration could ultimately prove a dead end.

The CMI and Post-CMI as Financial Cooperation Initiatives

One effect of the Asian financial crisis of 1997–98 was to lend new urgency to arguments that the region needed a mechanism through which countries could provide one another with short-term liquidity support.

---

[4] At the 6th Trilateral Finance Ministers' Meeting in Hyderabad in 2006.

In response, in May 2000, ASEAN+3 finance ministers agreed to create the CMI, to supplement existing international credit facilities and to address short-term balance of payment difficulties in the region. The CMI is an outgrowth and expansion of the ASEAN Swap Arrangements (ASA) established in 1977 through which ASEAN members provide one another with short-term swap facilities on a limited basis. The CMI, in contrast to this predecessor, encompasses not only the ASEAN countries but also China, Japan, and South Korea. It contains three financing schemes: (i) the ASA, (ii) a set of bilateral swap arrangements (BSAs), and (iii) a set of repurchase agreements. The ASA is a multilateral swap arrangement in the relatively modest amount of $1 billion. The BSAs among the various ASEAN+3 nations cover all 13 countries and amount to $84 billion (as of March 2008).[5] Finally, another $1 billion of short-term financial assistance can be extended through bilaterally organized repurchase agreements (For more details, see Appendices 3.1. and 3.2).

Under the provisions of the ASA, a participant can unilaterally refrain from providing financial assistance to a partner or partners. It merely has to inform the other participants of its decision. In the case of the BSAs, in contrast, a collective decision of whether to disburse is to be made following consultation among the swap-providing countries, with one of those countries serving as the coordinator. Disbursement of up to 20 percent of the maximum can occur without the country first reaching an agreement on a stabilization program with the International Monetary Fund (IMF). The BSA runs for 90 days and can be renewed for up to a maximum of two years. The interest rate is based on the London Interbank Offer Rate (LIBOR) and rises with the number of renewals. The original draw and first renewal are priced at 150 basis points over LIBOR. The rate then rises by 50 basis points for every two renewals. Thus, the BSA will be priced at 300 basis points over LIBOR by the time of the sixth and seventh renewals. Most BSAs are swaps of dollars for local currency, but Japan and China will use the yen and renminbi, respectively, in place of the dollar. There are no common rules governing other conditions such as credit risk, exchange risk, etc., the CMI leaving these aspects to the discretion of the lender and borrower.

---

[5] This is double the initially negotiated amount (see below).

Limitations of the CMI

Financial supports must be large relative to the resources that can be mobilized by private financial markets if they are to successfully repel speculative attacks. Even though the finance ministers of ASEAN+3 nations increased the BSAs from their initial $39.5 billion in 2000 to $84 billion as of early 2008, this amount is still limited compared to the vast liquidity of international capital markets.[6] In the Asian crisis of 1997–98, external financing packages for South Korea and Thailand alone reached US$50 billion, but this still fell far short of what was needed to maintain exchange rate and financial stability. And financial markets have grown rapidly over the intervening decade. Moreover, the amount that any one country can draw is only a fraction of the total so long as the swap lines are organized on a bilateral basis. For some countries (like China with international reserves approaching $2 trillion), the CMI system of swaps and credits is simply trivial.

An additional limitation is that drawings are not available automatically. In practice, each creditor has discretion over activation of its bilateral swap, reflecting the CMI's evolution out of the ASA, where this was similarly the practice. Even if swap contracts have been signed, engagement remains at the discretion of the creditor. The possibility of an opt-out makes the CMI unreliable as a source of timely support. It means that the mere existence of the CMI is not likely to deter speculators from taking positions against a currency. This problem can be solved only by compulsory engagement, but participating countries are not yet prepared to agree to such an arrangement.

Yet another limitation is conditionality. As noted above, as a condition for drawing most of the funds made available through the swaps, the borrower must have completed, or at least be nearing completion, an agreement with the IMF. That agreement will condition financing on a package of policy reforms to be instituted by the borrower. But it will be the IMF, and not the Asian countries themselves, that will decide the conditions.

This points to a final limitation having to do with speed. International Monetary Fund agreements take time to complete, and the resulting delay may mean that assistance through the CMI comes too late. Speed is of the essence in a crisis, it is not clear that the majority of the swaps and credits

---

[6] For more on this expansion, see below.

mobilized through the CMI can be dispersed within the necessary time frame.

These observations highlight the need for the CMI to create its own surveillance mechanism to free it from delays caused by negotiations with third parties like the Fund.[7] Ultimately, the existence of such a mechanism and its findings could provide the basis for lending conditions set down by the CMI countries themselves.

Some of these issues were addressed by ASEAN+3 finance ministers in 2004 and 2005, (see Fig. 3.1). At their 2005 meeting in Istanbul, Turkey, ASEAN+3 finance ministers enlarged the BSAs from $39.5 billion to $79 billion. They increased the ceiling for drawing on swaps that could be extended with prior negotiation of an IMF agreement from 10 percent to 20 percent.

Although these were limited steps toward creating a more autonomous and adequately funded CMI, they were indicative of the growth of self-confidence and solidarity among the participating governments. In the long run, an even more significant step was taken when ASEAN+3 finance ministers also agreed to develop the CMI into a multilateral "currency risk supporting system". The system was to be multilateral rather than bilateral in the sense that the financial resources committed by the participating countries would be effectively pooled. A working group was formed to explore ways of developing such a system and preparing terms of reference for a multilateral decision-making process. The following year that working group reported on the possible options to the 9th ASEAN+3 Financial Ministers' Meeting in Hyderabad, India. The Ministers endorsed its report and agreed to launch a task force responsible for the CMI's multilateralization. With this, the Post-CMI era began.

The Post-CMI

Table 3.1 summarizes the principal changes to the original CMI system. Participating countries will no longer be able to opt out in the event of activation. And rather than loaning currencies to one another bilaterally,

---

[7] The idea of institutionalizing ASEAN+3 surveillance has received a good deal of attention from academics and others: see Kawai (2002; 2005), Girardin (2004), and Rajan and Sireger (2004).

[May 2000] **Chiang Mai Initiative (CMI): Inception**

[2004/05] **CMI review WG** to enhance its effectiveness on the **Jeju Agreement 2004 (first-phase review)**

[May 2005] **Istanbul Agreement after the first review—CMI second stage**
- Integration of economic surveillance into the CMI
- Adoption of collective decision-making mechanism
- Significant increase in size of swaps
- Improving the drawdown mechanism (10 → 20%) and maintenance of disciplined terms of swap

[2005/06] **CMI review WG (second-phase review)**

1. Documentation of the Istanbul Agreement
- Revision/Conclusion of BSAs
- Amendment of Basic Framework and Main Principles

2. Issues carried over from the first phase (2004/05)
- Swap activation process—Incorporation ofTOR into main principles
- Enhancement of surveillance—Regional expertise

3. Medium- to long-term issues
- Further use of ASEAN+3 local currencies
- Multilateralizing the CMI

[May 2006] AFMM+3 in Hyderabad, India
- Agreement and endorsement of the CMI WG (Phase II)
- Completion of CMI review process
- Agreed launch of new task force for CMI's multilateralization: Post-CMI

[May 2007] AFMM+3 in Kyoto, Japan
- Multilateralization of CMI proceeded
- Strengthened cooperation on regional surveillance alongside CMI

Figure 3.1. Overview of the CMI's development.

the monies will be drawn from pooled reserves. There are two pooling arrangements: upfront funding and self-managed reserve pooling. Upfront funding means that each central bank transfers a part of its reserves to a regional fund. Those reserves will, of course, have to be managed, which

Table 3.1. CMI vs. Post-CMI.

Criteria	CMI	Post-CMI
Form	BSAs	Reserve pooling
Size of commitments	Voluntary	Voluntary/By Rules
Amount of funding	By BSAs	By total contribution
Multiplying effect	None	Possible
Activation	By negotiation	Central body
Amount of drawing	Proportional to bilateral commitment	Proportional to contribution
Opt-out option	Possible	None
Uniformity agreement	Multiple agreements	Single agreement
Coordination mechanism	Bilateral	Multilateral
Reserve volume	Reduced after activation	Preserved
Surveillance	IMF conditionality	Internal institution

will in turn require the CMI to develop additional administrative capacity. To be sure, this administrative capacity will not be cheap or easy to develop, either economically or politically. But it is likely to provide an impetus for institution building. Moreover, this pool of paid-in funds can be deployed for a variety of purposes related to efforts to deepen international monetary cooperation (as described below).

With self-managed reserve pooling, the participating countries pledge reserves to a coordinator. This is purely an accounting transaction; countries do not have to transfer reserves until the need to lend them arises. This method has the advantage of limiting administrative costs and is easier politically, although it provides less impetus for transnational institution building.

At the 10th AFMM in Kyoto in 2007, it was then agreed "that a self-managed reserve pooling arrangement governed by a single contractual agreement is an appropriate form of multilateralization".[8] But the participants did not decide on commitment size, borrowing quota, activation mechanism, administrative structure, or other institutional aspects of their arrangement. The devil, as they say, is in the details, which will determine

---

[8] This followed a decision taken at the 9th AFMM+3 meeting. At Kyoto, ministers instructed their deputies to conduct further in-depth studies of these further detailed aspects of the agreement.

whether the multilateralized Post-CMI evolves into a true transnational regional body capable of fostering regional monetary and financial integration or it remains only a loose inter-governmental organization.

The 10th AFMM also "reaffirmed the importance and necessity of strengthening cooperation on regional surveillance alongside the CMI multilateralization process".[9] A Group of Experts (GOE) and a Technical Working Group on Economic and Financial Monitoring (ETWG) will be responsible for assessing economic conditions in the participating countries.[10] The Economic Review and Policy Dialog group established by the 6th AFMM in 2003 will provide a further venue for exchanges of views among policymakers.

The need to strengthen surveillance is related to the desire to free the arrangement from IMF surveillance and conditionality. If the participating countries can exercise firm surveillance of one another, then there will no longer be a need to delegate the surveillance function to the Fund. But a necessary condition for constructive policy dialog and effective coordination is the availability of reliable information. Sharing information can enhance the welfare of other countries insofar as better information leads to more efficient policy decisions. Sharing information in a joint forum would also apply "peer pressure" for individual countries to avoid policies that may be harmful for others — and even for themselves.[11] Relying on individual countries to provide that information may not work, however, because governments have an incentive to withhold or disguise information that places them in an unfavorable light. This creates a need for an independent monitor. A global monitor already exists, namely the IMF. But a specialized regional monitor like the GOE or ETWG may be able to process information on the Asian economies more efficiently than a global monitor. But to do these jobs effectively, the GOE and ETWG need to develop continuity and institutional memory. In other words, they need to be able to evolve into a self-standing surveillance organization with an independent secretariat and an autonomous, adequately compensated management and staff.

---

[9] From the official statement of the 10th AFMM+3 Meeting in Kyoto in 2007.

[10] Different options to constitute the surveillance unit are under discussion. For the details of GOE and ETWG, refer to the official 9th AFMM+3 statement, issued in Hyderabad in 2006.

[11] See Monteil (2004), pp. 7–12.

Toward a RCU

Another problem with the CMI is its reliance on the dollar as the counterpart currency for most of its local currency swaps. An arrangement designed to enhance East Asia's monetary and financial self-reliance may end up heightening the region's dependence on the dollar. Wider use of a regional currency is one way of surmounting this problem and enhancing the effectiveness of the Post-CMI.

Authors have advanced the case for a regional currency as an anchor for exchange-rate cooperation (Moon *et al.*, 2000), as a unit of denomination in regional bond markets (Ogawa and Shimizu, 2006), and as an indicator to be used for regional surveillance (Adams and Chow, 2007). The idea of developing a RCU was embraced by the Asian Development Bank (ADB) in 2005. The finance ministers of China, Japan, and South Korea called for further research on mechanisms for developing an RCU in their 6th Trilateral Finance Ministers' Meeting in 2006. The ASEAN+3 Research Group also has been analyzing this issue for several years.[12]

The RCU would be a weighted average of national currencies. Thus, the simplest approach to using the RCU in surveillance would be to adopt it as a divergence indicator. When the difference between the relative price of the RCU and a national currency implicit in the RCU weighting system and the actual exchange rate became too large, the need for corrective action would be signaled.

The RCU could also provide a stepping-stone to monetary union if it came into active use throughout the region. (This would be an application of the parallel-currency approach to monetary integration described by Eichengreen in Chapter 2.) The question is how to encourage its active use. One obvious answer is by utilizing it in the Post-CMI, where it could be adopted as the denomination currency for paid-in commitments and short- and medium-term liquidity support. The RCU could also be used as the unit of account for loans extended by the ADB to member countries, which would also encourage wider use and foster familiarity.

---

[12] The ASEAN+3 Research Group is constituted by the AFMM. With the support of two other members, a participating country suggests a research issue to be pursued in the AFMM. If its suggestion is accepted, a research group made up of experts in the region is then constituted. The country that tabled the proposal underwrites the expenses of ASEAN researchers. The two supporting countries finance the expenses of their participants. The research group then makes a report to the AFMM in the following year.

The RCU could also be used in conjunction with a future East Asian exchange-rate mechanism. Imagine that East Asian countries decide to create a multilateral exchange-rate system along the lines of the Exchange-Rate Mechanism (ERM) of the European Monetary System (EMS), as described by Moon and Rhee in their chapter in this volume. This system would require credit facilities similar to those that European countries provided to one another under the ERM's very short-term financing facility. When the bilateral exchange rate reached its upper or lower limit of fluctuation, the central banks issuing the two currencies would be called upon to intervene. Their intervention obligations and repayment of the credits extended through their short-term financing facilities could be denominated in and settled in RCU.

Ultimately, the RCU could be used not only as the unit of account but also as a means of payment. But this would require the RCU to be issued by a regional institution, which might be called the Asian Monetary Cooperation Fund (AMCF), analogously to how the IMF issues Special Drawing Rights, which can be thought of as a global parallel currency. The RCU could be backed by foreign exchange reserves, including gold, dollars and euros, subscribed by the countries that are shareholders in the AMCF. Alternatively, it could be backed by local currencies. In this case, each central bank would transfer a certain amount of its currency to the AMCF and receive RCUs in return according to the central RCU exchange rate. If the RCU was issued against national currencies, intervention at the bilateral margins could be conducted in a centralized manner: the central banks involved in the intervention would be indirectly, rather than directly, linked through the AMCF. Borrowing and lending of reserves in RCU among central banks in the region would occur through the AMCF's mediation.

What would be the relationship between the Post-CMI and the AMCF? The Post-CMI aims to provide an emergency help — including a monitoring and surveillance system — for countries suffering financial crises. An AMCF — as envisaged here — would be charged with issuing and managing the RCU with the aim of fostering exchange-rate stability. Clearly, these two sets of functions are related. If a currency reaches the edge of its fluctuation band and market participants begin to doubt whether the national authorities can prevent it from straying further, the result may be not just a currency crisis but a financial crisis as well. This would be a twin crisis in whose management both the Post-CMI and AMCF would play a role. Coordination being difficult, there is thus an argument for rolling the two entities into a single organization, which might be called, political sensitivities permitting, the Asian Monetary Fund.

The RCU as a Catalyst for Financial Market Development

For the RCU to provide a stepping-stone to the monetary union, it will have to come into active private use. The most obvious way this can come about is as a unit of denomination for financial products. The RCU, as a composite currency, has natural attractions as a financial unit. Exchange-rate fluctuations are a deterrent to cross-border financial transactions. If the transaction is denominated in the borrower's currency, then the lender shoulders the exchange risk, and vice versa. Exchange risk can be hedged, but only at a cost. And even if it is hedged, that open foreign currency position will be passed on to someone else, like a domestic bank that ends up with the open position as a result. In any case, because hedging markets do not exist at long maturities, some long-lived instruments like long-term bonds cannot be hedged in this manner.

A proliferation of national currencies is thus a deterrent to more active cross-border investment, resulting in the continued fragmentation of Asian bond markets. It is no coincidence that the largest and most liquid bond markets are those of the United States and the Euro area, the two largest monetary unions in the world. It follows that Asia's failure to move more quickly in the direction of monetary union or at least strong exchange-rate coordination is an obstacle to the development of a deep and liquid regional bond market.

The development of a composite currency can help to address these problems. It would reduce the exchange risk incurred by investors insofar as it is more stable against the component currencies than they are against each other. Additionally, the interest rate of a composite currency is the weighted average of its constituent currencies. Therefore, a borrower in a country whose interest rate is relatively high may gain by borrowing in RCU, and an investor in a country whose interest rate is relatively low may be better off by investing in RCU. These advantages explain the rapid growth of the issuance of bonds and international bank credits denominated in ECUs in Europe in the 1980s.[13]

---

[13] Some authors argue, however, that it is mainly German regulation limiting the issuance of deutsche mark-denominated bonds that explains the popularity in this period of ECU-denominated bonds (Dammers and McCauley, 2006).

Privately created RCU can also be used as a means of payment. An investor acquiring RCU-denominated bonds can pay in RCUs by asking his/her bank to change his/her deposits from the national currency to RCUs. To satisfy this request, the bank has to obtain RCUs by purchasing constituent currencies in the exchange market and transferring them to the issuer's bank account. In doing so, the bank creates private RCUs.

The firm issuing the bonds and receiving the RCU payment can either keep the deposits in RCUs or ask its bank to transfer the RCUs as deposits in a certain currency. In the latter case, RCUs exist only ephemerally. However, because the coupon also must be paid in RCUs, there will be ongoing use of the private RCU. Moreover, in cases where the issuer keeps the deposits in RCU, the bank will keep the constituent currencies as assets and RCU deposits as liabilities on the balance sheet.

If the operation proceeds as described above, there is no exchange-rate risk for either bank. However, creating RCUs by purchasing constituent currencies or by eliminating RCUs by selling them entails transactions costs. Therefore, the scenario described above is unlikely. But as the issuance of financial claims denominated in RCU increases, there may appear a bank (call it "Bank A") that is willing to play the role of market maker for RCU. When another bank ("Bank B") needs RCUs, it can purchase them directly from Bank A in exchange for a currency (typically the national currency of Bank B). When Bank B has acquired RCUs, it can sell them to Bank A in exchange for a currency (again, typically the national currency of Bank B). The risk to banks other than the market maker will be reduced by this netting of credits and debits. The market maker, for its part, can earn fee income in exchange for assuming the exchange risk.

In Europe, Denmark's Kredietbank initially took on the role of market maker for ECU. As time passed, this function was also performed by other banks such as Lloyds in the United Kingdom. These market maker banks bought and sold ECU at a modest spread over the official rate. Competition among them limited the fee income that they could charge and made it more economical for other banks to net their credits and debits. A money market in ECU thus developed naturally, given that a bank with an abundance of ECU had an incentive to lend to banks in need of ECU. Before long the interbank market in ECU became one of the largest segments of the Eurocurrency markets.

Banks functioning as market makers for ECU also provided clearing and settlement services for other banks. Clearing and settlement among banks that did not have accounts at the same clearing bank occurred via bilateral or multilateral agreements among clearing banks. On September 17, 1985, 18 banks that maintained an interest in the development of ECU transactions and in their clearing and settlement established the ECU Banking Association (EBA). Commercial banks kept their ECU accounts at the clearing banks of the EBA.

What can East Asian countries do to encourage similar developments? Above all, they can take steps to encourage more active private use of the RCU. To start with, they can provide a clear official definition of the RCU in order to encourage the markets to organize themselves around that unit rather than around one or more competing composite currencies that might develop spontaneously. The coexistence of several private RCUs would fragment the market, diminish the liquidity of each, and render private RCUs less attractive to potential market makers.

Second, governments and regional organizations can issue RCU-denominated bonds. In Europe, the European Investment Bank and national governments raised funds by issuing ECU bonds or borrowing from banks in ECU. The ADB and Asian governments could take similar actions.

Third, stabilizing exchange rates among the constituent currencies would encourage private use of the RCU by enhancing the predictability of the domestic-currency value of returns on RCU-denominated bonds. This observation explains why the development of ECU-denominated financial markets slowed after the crisis in the EMS, which increased the uncertainty surrounding exchange rates between national currencies and the ECU. This observation suggests that the parallel-currency approach to monetary integration is not an alternative to exchange-rate stabilization; rather, the two approaches should proceed in tandem. The challenge, of course, is the difficulty of stabilizing exchange rates in a world of high capital mobility such as that which prevails in East Asia today.

Fourth, an efficient and a reliable clearing and settlement system for private RCU claims is essential. In Europe, the clearing and settlement of ECU-denominated bank claims was based on three institutions: the European Banking Association, the Bank for International Settlements (BIS), and the Society for Worldwide Interbank Financial Telecommunication (SWIFT). The BIS signed an agreement with the European Banking Association under which it assumed the role of agent for clearing and settlement on behalf of clearing banks. Transactions among clearing banks of the European Banking Association then took place through transfers across accounts (ECUCOVER accounts) held at the BIS. Other commercial banks used the clearing banks' accounts for settlement in ECU. Daily messages on payments were transmitted through the SWIFT network. The clearing system gradually opened to the addition of new clearing banks, whose number exceeded 80 by the 1990s. The BIS assured the reliability of the system by assuming the function of supervisor despite the fact that it did not provide liquidity assistance.[14]

Clearing and settlement of RCU funds in Asia could follow the European model. Banks could establish an association and a clearing arrangement. To assure the credibility of the clearing system, it would be desirable for a public organization, such as the Hong Kong branch of the BIS or ADB, to support the initiative. Alternatively, the banks forming an association could establish a private institution to manage clearing accounts on behalf of the association. There may be a rivalry as to where the new institution should be located, but there is no major technical or institutional obstacle to the introduction of the settlement system for RCU inter-bank claims.

Devising a settlement system for RCU-denominated securities is more complicated than the settlement of inter-bank claims, since settlement of a securities transaction involves not just the payment of funds between buyer and seller but also the delivery of securities. Therefore, it is essential to establish settlement procedures that only allow securities to be delivered to the buyer on condition of payment being received by the seller (to establish a system of delivery versus payment, or DVP, in other words). Efficient cross-border settlement further requires the harmonization of different technical requirements, market practices, tax regimes, and legal systems because it involves counterparties residing in different countries. Indeed, even European countries are still struggling to establish a Europe-wide securities settlement system.[15] One option is to use the existing international central securities depositories (ICSD) such as Euroclear or Clearstream International. However, it is not clear whether those ICSDs would offer settlement in RCUs even before RCU securities took off (Eichengreen, 2007c). Moreover, the fact that these ICSDs are located in Europe is a drawback because investors in Asia would lose

---

[14] Refer to Giovanoli (1989) for more details about the role of the BIS relating to the ECU.
[15] See Giovannini Group (2001; 2003). The authors maintain that European countries' securities settlement system is fragmented so that international investment involves important costs and risks.

liquidity for an additional day: to get the settlement in $T + 2$ days, the buyer has to send the settlement funds in $T + 1$.

For all these reasons, it would be desirable to develop an Asia-based alternative on either a centralized or decentralized basis. In a centralized system, each national central securities depository (NCSD) would be connected to a newly created Asian central securities depository. The decentralized system would consist of a network of bilateral connections among NCSDs in the region. Competition among NCSDs in a decentralized system would provide impetus for greater efficiency. But a centralized system would be better positioned to reap the scale economies created by the existence of network externalities in settlement. Connecting the various NCSDs would also be costly and technically difficult, as there is no standard settlement platform for different NCSDs. It is uncertain whether Asia would be able to establish a harmonized platform through a decentralized process. Thus, it seems that a "big-bang" approach toward a centralized system is the more desirable alternative for Asia (Chai and Rhee, 2005).

Fifth, capital account liberalization is an important condition for wider use of the RCU. Deregulation and opening of domestic financial systems are necessary to permit domestic investors to invest in foreign bonds and otherwise hold their savings in foreign currency. Here again, European experience is instructive. Many European countries in the 1980s retained substantial restrictions on capital flows, and those restrictions limited the development of financial markets in ECU. Only after the Single European Act and two related Council directives in the late 1980s did the liberalization of capital flows acquire significant momentum in Europe. Before that, the bulk of financial transactions in ECU was on Eurocurrency and Eurobond markets. In Asia, RCU-denominated financial markets equivalent to Eurocurrency or Eurobond markets could develop even if substantial capital controls are maintained. But for the RCU to be utilized more widely, it would be necessary to liberalize capital flows.

A final policy to encourage wider use of the RCU would be to give it discharging power in payment or, more powerfully, legal tender status for domestic transactions. As Eichengreen (2007c, p. 153) explains:

"... Asian countries are reluctant to give the currency of an outside power legal tender status for domestic transactions ... Under the parallel currency approach, Asian governments would give [the RCU] full legal tender status; they would also authorize it for domestic use, in other words, which would make it more attractive."

But whether governments will be prepared anytime soon to take this momentous step is unclear. Countries with weak currencies might be especially reluctant to give legal tender status to an alternative, fearing seigniorage losses.[16] A technical solution would be for the AMCF to provide a guarantee against the depreciation of the RCU when issued against national currencies. If a currency depreciates, the concerned country could transfer more units of its currency to the AMCF as a counterpart of the RCU to keep the exchange rate of the RCU stable vis-à-vis the strongest currency. This is similar to the solution proposed by the British government under the name "hard ECU" in the early 1990s.[17] The proposal was favorably received by other countries but rejected by the European Commission on the grounds that it was too complicated technically.[18] A "hard RCU" was would be even more complicated if it was not accompanied by a regional exchange-rate arrangement comparable to that which existed in Europe in the 1980s. Exchange rates would be fluctuating continuously, requiring continuous compensatory transactions, rather than being devalued and revalued at long intervals. Again, the difficulty of stabilizing exchange rates in a world of high capital mobility raises doubts about the feasibility of a hard-RCU scheme.

Conclusion

Since the financial crisis of 1997–98, there have been ongoing discussions and a series of initiatives to encourage monetary cooperation and develop financial markets in East Asia. However, monetary and financial initiatives have been pursued independently without regard for or consideration

---

[16] Countries with strong currencies might be more willing to do so, but there the RCU may not be able to compete with the national unit.

[17] See Grice (1990).

[18] One of the technical questions raised was whether the basket should be modified whenever there is devaluation of a currency.

of their implications for one another. Our message in this chapter is that more attention needs to be paid to the connections and inter-relationships between the two.

The most prominent initiative in the financial sphere is the CMI for addressing the problems of financial instability. The challenge going forward is not only to expand its financial capacity but also to develop effective surveillance and macroeconomic policy coordination mechanisms. While there is much work to be done to attain these goals, it is not unreasonable to see this initiative as a stepping-stone toward a truly multilateral regional institution for dealing with problems of financial instability — as an embryonic "Asian Monetary Fund".

But financial stability cannot be achieved without systematic and effective monetary cooperation. Two approaches have been widely discussed in this context: schemes for stabilizing intra-regional exchange rates and issuing a parallel currency or RCU. The RCU exchange rate can be used as a divergence indicator in surveillance. For purposes of exchange-rate coordination, the RCU can become an anchor currency and a means of payment. It may also reduce reliance in the region on external currencies like the US dollar. Finally, as the RCU is used more widely in private transactions, it can pave the way to the eventual creation of a single Asian currency.

But simply defining the RCU will not be enough to encourage its active private use. Use of the RCU in official transactions and, more importantly, an exchange-rate coordination system are needed to foster the development of private markets in the RCU. The parallel currency and exchange-rate stabilization approaches to monetary cooperation in Asia are not alternatives or substitutes. Rather, they are complementary and should be pursued in tandem.

Appendix 3.1: BSAs Under CMI as of End of 2006

[Total: 16 BSAs, US$ 77.0 billion]

Countries		Currencies	Size	Date of conclusion and expiry	N.B.
China → Indonesia	One-way	US$/Rupiah	US$ 4 billion	Concluded/17 October 2006 [Expiry/16 October 2009]	Second stage
China ↔ Japan	Two-way	Renminbi/ Yen Yen/ Renminbi	US$ 3 billion *2	Concluded/28 March 2002 [Expiry/27 March 2006]	
China ↔ Korea	Two-way	Renminbi/ Won Won/ Renminbi	US$ 4 billion *2	Revised/27 May 2005 [Expiry/23 June 2007]	Second stage
China → Malaysia	One-way	US$/Ringgit	US$ 1.5 billion	Concluded/9 October 2002 [Expiry/8 October 2005]	Expired, but under negotiation for extension
China → Philippines	One-way	Renminbi/ Peso	US$ 1 billion	Concluded/29 August 2003 [Expiry/28 August 2006]	
China → Thailand	One-way	US$/Baht	US$ 2 billion	Concluded/6 December 2001 [Expiry/5 December 2004]	Expired, but under negotiation for extension
Indonesia ← Japan	One-way	US$/Rupiah	US$ 6 billion	Concluded/31 August 2005 [Expiry/30 August 2008]	Second stage

(Continued)

Appendix 3.1: (*Continued*)

Countries	Currencies	Size	Date of conclusion and expiry	N.B.
Indonesia ↔ Korea	Two-way	US$/Won US$/ Rupiah	US$ 1 billion *2	Concluded/24 December 2003 [Expiry/23 December 2006]	
Japan ↔ Korea	Two-way	US$/Won US$/Yen	US$ 10 billion US$ 5 billion	Concluded/24 February 2006 [Expiry/23 February 2009]	Second stage
Japan ↔ Korea	Two-way	US$/Won US$/Yen	US$ 3 billion *2	Concluded/27 May 2005 [Expiry/3 July 2007]	
Japan → Malaysia	One-way	US$/Ringgit	US$ 1 billion	Concluded/5 October 2001 [Expiry/4 October 2007]	Under negotiation to incorporate 2005 AFMM+3 decisions
Japan ↔ Philippines	Two-way	US$/Peso US$/Yen	US$ 6 billion US$ 500 million	Concluded/4 May 2006 [Expiry/3 May 2009]	Second stage
Japan ↔ Singapore	Two-way	US$/SG$ US$/Yen	US$ 3 billion US$ 1 billion	Concluded/8 November 2005 [Expiry/7 November 2008]	Second stage
Japan ↔ Thailand	Two-way	US$/Baht US$/Yen	US$ 3 billion *2	Concluded/7 March 2005 [Expiry/6 March 2007]	Second stage

(*Continued*)

Appendix 3.1: *(Continued)*

Countries		Currencies	Size	Date of conclusion and expiry	N.B.
Korea ↔ Malaysia	Two-way	US$/Ringgit US$/Won	US$ 1.5 billion *2	Concluded/14 October 2005 [Expiry/13 October 2008]	Second stage
Korea ↔ Philippines	Two-way	US$/Peso US$/Won	US$ 1.5 billion *2	Concluded/17 October 2005 [Expiry/16 October 2007]	Second stage
Korea ↔ Thailand	Two-way	US$/Baht US$/Won	US$ 1 billion *2	Concluded/12 December 2005 [Expiry/11 December 2007]	Second stage

Appendix 3.2: Comparison of Swap Arrangements and Facilities.

Arrangement of facility	Origin	Size	Terms	Decision on activation	Conditionality	Surveillance
European short-term facilities	Stabilization of intra-European exchange rates, 1972; creation of the EMS, 1979	Potentially unlimited in the very short term, but effectively subject to Bundesbank's acquiescence. Renewals were limited by quotas, initially ECU7.9 billion.	75 days, renewable twice for 3 months, at market interest rates	Automatic when the exchange rate reached the margin.	None at the initial drawing; but potential conditions on renewals beyond 6 months. Moreover, Germany exercised pressure for convergence toward low inflation.	Originally, EC surveillance was weak, then was strengthened in the 1990s.
European medium-term facility	Community obligations and Werner Plan, 1971	ECU 16 billion; now reduces to €12 billion	2 to 5 years set by Ecofin Council, as was interest rate	Ecofin Council decision	Yes; set by Ecofin Council	See above

(Continued)

Appendix 3.2: (*Continued*)

Arrangement of facility	Origin	Size	Terms	Decision on activation	Conditionality	Surveillance
North American Framework Agreement	NAFTA implementation in 1994	About $8.6 billion total	3 months, renewable at least up to 1 year; 91-day T-bill rate	Two-key	Informal and indirect	Through IMF and NAFG
CMI	Reaction to Asian financial crisis, 2000	Expected to exceed $25 billion when completed	3 months; renewable up to 2 years; CCL interest rates	Two-key	Applied through IMF link	Regional mechanism in early stages of development; mainly through IMF

Notes: CCL = Contingent Credit Line; EC = European Community; ECU = European Currency Unit; EMS = European Monetary System; NAFG = North American Financial Group and NAFTA = North American Free Trade Agreement.

CHAPTER 4

Financial Integration and Exchange-Rate Coordination in East Asia

Woosik Moon and Yeongseop Rhee

Introduction

In a world of deeply integrated financial markets, emerging-market economies are susceptible to capital flow surges, sudden stops, and other manifestations of volatility in international financial markets. Options for dealing with these problems are limited. Impermeable capital controls are not feasible given the liberalization of domestic financial markets and the desire for regional financial integration. Freely floating exchange rates are not acceptable to countries that see currency stability as conducive to the expansion of their exports and integral to growth. Indicative of this, many countries in East Asia continue to intervene heavily to stabilize their currencies despite the challenges posed by the expansion of international financial markets and growth of capital flows.

Exchange-rate stability cannot be achieved without cost. This cost is likely to be highest when countries attempt to stabilize their currencies unilaterally. In a collective exchange-rate arrangement (when several countries attempt to stabilize against one another), there will always be a strong-currency country with excess reserves that can be lent to its weak-currency counterpart. In effect, regional monetary cooperation acts as a form of coinsurance, limiting the costs of stabilization.

The countries of East Asia have become so interdependent economically that the need for some form of exchange-rate coordination is undeniable. Exchange-rate coordination may also be helpful for relieving the stresses created by payments imbalances between Asia and other regions: it provides a mechanism for solving the first-mover problem that threatens to stifle adjustment. If one country allows its currency to appreciate against the US dollar in order to cut its external surplus and slow its accumulation of reserves but others keep their dollar exchange rates unchanged, the initiating country may suffer a damaging loss of competiveness. It will lose competiveness not just in the US market but in other Asian markets as well. The consequences will then be viewed as too costly to justify making a national contribution to global rebalancing. But if all Asian countries move simultaneously, the same overall contribution to global rebalancing can be achieved without any Asian currency having to move against the dollar by more than a modest amount. In addition, no Asian country will lose competitiveness against its regional neighbors. This provides another rationale for a mechanism to foster monetary cooperation in East Asia, this being the principal surplus region in the world.

The remainder of this chapter considers the limits to unilateral exchange-rate stabilization and the advantages of regional monetary cooperation in more detail. It quantifies those costs in an emerging East Asian country, taking South Korea as its example. It highlights the advantages of regional monetary and exchange-rate coordination. It then observes how growing appreciation of these advantages has begun to lead to advances in the areas of monetary and financial cooperation, notably the creation of a regional currency unit and the provision of emergency liquidity assistance under the provisions of the Chiang Mai Initiative (CMI). The implication is that exchange-rate coordination is logically the next agenda item to be addressed.

Growing Interdependence is an Asian Reality

Intra-Asian trade and investment have been trending upward now for several decades. This trend was disrupted by the crisis of 1997–98 — which disrupted virtually everything in the region — but then resumed even more strongly with the post-crisis recovery (see Fig. 4.1). The same has been true of intra-regional foreign direct investment (FDI) flows: these too have been rising strongly in recent years, especially flows to China from other middle- and high-income Asian economies such as South Korea, Taiwan, Singapore, and Japan.

The growth of intra-Asian trade and FDI points to the desirability of stable exchange rates within the region. The fact that Asian countries compete with one another in third markets points in the same direction. As South Korea came to compete more and more with Japan in international

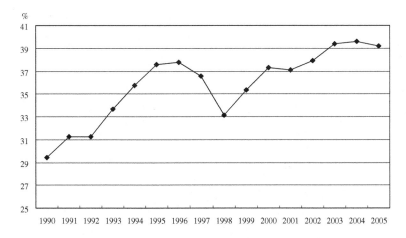

Figure 4.1. Intra-regional trade share in East Asia (ASEAN+3).
Source: Asian Development Bank, *Asia Regional Integration Center Database.*

Table 4.1. Frankel and Wei regressions.

	Korea		Thailand		Indonesia		Philippines	
	1990–96	1999–2005	1990–96	1999–2005	1990–96	1999–2005	1990–96	1999–2005
$\beta1$	0.9161	0.4652	0.8250	0.3592	0.9779	—	1.1087	0.7973
	(0.040)	(0.276)	(0.010)	(0.175)	(0.011)	0.2065	(0.094)	(0.069)
						(0.548)		
$\beta2$	0.0949	0.5863	0.1057	0.3939	0.0113	0.6779	−0.1103	0.2227
	(0.032)	(0.194)	(0.009)	(0.159)	(0.011)	(0.409)	(0.056)	(0.082)

Source: Kim and Jeong (2006).
Note: β_1 and β_2 denote the coefficients of the dollar and the yen, respectively in the regression. The number in parentheses is the standard deviation.

markets, for example, Korean exporters and officials alike became much more conscious of the won-yen exchange rate. Table 4.1 shows that most Asian countries continuing to actively manage their exchange rates in the post-crisis period saw their currencies become increasingly linked to the yen (see Kim and Jeong, 2006).[1] Even in China, which so far has been

---

[1] The principal exceptions being China and Malaysia.

reluctant to commit intellectually to the idea of region-wide exchange and monetary coordination, there is an increasing awareness of the desirability of the goal of intra-regional exchange-rate stability.

Compared to trade and FDI flows, portfolio capital flows and the integration of debt and equity markets have proceeded more gradually (Cowen *et al.*, 2007; Kawai, 2007a). However, integration has now accelerated in response to policy reforms at the national level and regional measures such as the Asian Bond Fund and the Asian Bond Market Initiative. The resulting short-term capital flows are tying economic conditions in different East Asian countries increasingly tightly together.

Figure 4.2 shows capital inflows and outflows in eight East Asian countries.[2] Cross-border bank loans have been the single most important component of those flows. Loans rose sharply following the crisis, partly in reflection of their collapse in the earlier period. This rebound was then followed by an equally sharp increase in cross-border debt and equity flows. These developments deepened financial links not only among East Asian countries but also their financial links with the United States and Europe, given that a substantial fraction of debt and equity flows were inter-regional. Emerging East Asian financial markets became increasingly integrated not just with one another but also with major global financial centers such as New York and London, in other words. (Figure 4.3 summarizes the recent behavior of the US and Japanese bank lending to Asia.)

To be sure, capital controls were maintained by some countries, China and Malaysia prominent among them, limiting portfolio flows and financial-market integration to lower levels than would have prevailed otherwise. But given the search for yield, market participants found ways around these controls. Short-term capital movements increased strongly, mainly as a result of banks searching for higher yields. Focusing on errors and omissions in the balance of payments, Goodfriend and Prasad (2005) have argued that even China has seen its capital account open and its exposure to short-term capital flows increase substantially in recent years. Using a different methodology, Ma and McCauley (2007) reached essentially the same conclusion.

Since 2003, there have been growing capital outflows from Japan, particularly in the form of loans by Japanese banks (Fig. 4.4). These

---

[2] These include Korea, Japan, China, and the most advanced ASEAN 5 countries (Indonesia, Malaysia, the Philippines, Singapore, and Thailand).

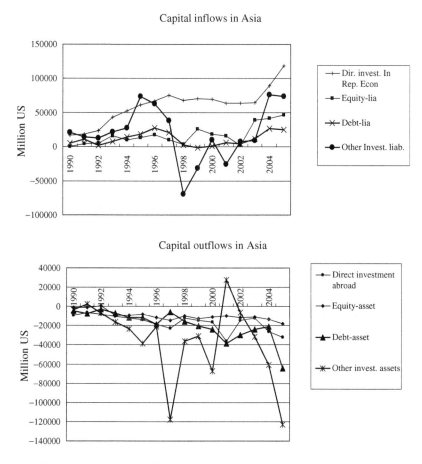

Figure 4.2. Capital flows in East Asia (8 countries) 1990–2005.
Source: International Monetary Fund, *International Financial Statistics*.
Note: Other investment liabilities and assets consist largely of commercial borrowings and loans.

flows — known as the yen carry trade — were motivated by the low level of interest rates in Japan. Japanese banks could fund themselves at low cost, since the interest rates they had to pay depositors and on the money market were relatively low, and then turn around and use the proceeds to invest in assets denominated in other higher-yielding currencies. Figure 4.5 shows the divergences in interest rates across East Asian countries motivating the carry trade.

The claims of the US banks on East Asian countries

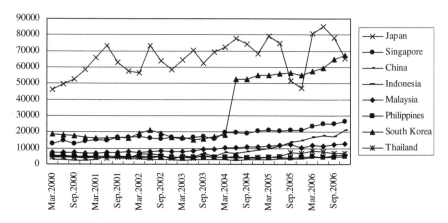

The claims of the Japanese banks on East Asian countries

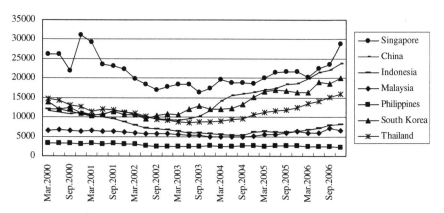

Figure 4.3. Claims of the US and Japanese banks on East Asian countries (million US dollars).
Source: Bank for International Settlements (http://www.bis.org/statistics/bankstats.htm).

The assumption implicit in this investment strategy was that exchange rates would remain stable — that appreciation of the yen would not wipe out gains from the carry trade. Thus, the exchange-rate regime is an important part of the carry-trade story. This points to an important corollary — that countries can insulate themselves from the dislocations caused by

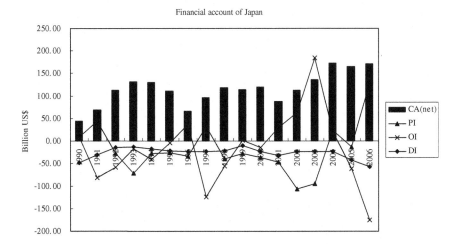

Figure 4.4. Japan's capital account.
Source: International Monetary Fund, *International Financial Statistics*.
Note: CA, PI, OI, and DI denote respectively current account, portfolio investment, other investments that are largely commercial loans and borrowings, and
direct investment.

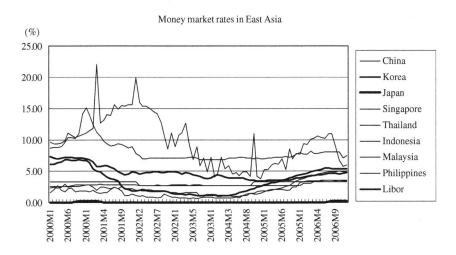

Figure 4.5. Interest rates in East Asia.
Source: International Monetary Fund, *International Financial Statistics*.

short-term capital flows by adopting more exchange-rate variability so as to discourage the carry trade. This creates an obvious tension, however, with the desire for and proposals to attain exchange-rate stability within Asia. At the same time, it is a reminder that in a world of higher capital mobility, the main options for exchange-rate management will be relatively free floating on one hand and a collective commitment to firmly pegging currencies on the other (more on this below).

These intra-regional capital movements have been a source of tension and economic difficulty. They have forced countries on the receiving end to choose between an autonomous monetary policy appropriate for domestic economic conditions and a stable exchange rate against the dollar. The growth of capital mobility and the so-called "trilemma" of international macroeconomics — that a country cannot have open capital markets, monetary autonomy, and exchange-rate stability all at the same time — has forced them to choose so.

The carry trade survived the Asian currency crisis, presumably because interest rates remained low in Japan, reflecting that country's still sluggish growth. But not everything else remained the same; in particular, Asian countries that were running current account deficits and importing capital to finance high levels of investment before the crisis shifted to current account surplus and to exporting capital subsequently. They ran their economies under less pressure of demand, given the lesson that an excessive pressure could lead to the build-up of financial vulnerabilities. As a result, they accumulated massive amounts of foreign reserves, which were seen as a bulwark against another crisis. Asian central banks and governments turned around and invested those reserves in the US government and agency securities, and US banks then recycled these investments by making their own bank loans to and underwriting FDI by companies setting up in East Asia (Park and Yang, 2006). Together with tax cuts and the accommodating monetary policies of the Bush Presidency and the Greenspan Fed, which stimulated demand and fed current account deficits in the United States, this explains the pattern of global imbalances that we have seen in recent years.

In this world of rapidly rising short-term capital flows, it has become difficult for East Asian countries to keep their exchange rates from moving on. They have had to pay significant and rising costs when intervening in the foreign exchange market to stabilize their currencies, as we show in the following paragraphs.

Although this experience is common across the region, Korea's case is especially dramatic. More than any other East Asian country, Korea threw open the capital account following the crisis. There was a burgeoning of short-term capital inflows (in particular, a substantial increase in loans from foreign banks). There was also interest arbitrage by foreign bank subsidiaries and domestic banks, as well as by some non-residents, all of which contributed to capital flows (see below).

Intervention Costs

Since the crisis, East Asian central banks have intervened extensively in foreign exchange markets to limit the movement of their currencies. Although they are not always explicit about the objective, the goal, broadly speaking, has been to maintain the growth of exports and keep the current account in surplus as part of what has come to be called the Asian growth model.

As pointed out by Mohanty and Turner (2005), such interventions are costly. Interest rates tend to be higher in fast-growing emerging markets than in the major financial centers. Recall our discussion of the yen carry trade above, although the point applies more widely. It even applies to China now that Chinese interest rates have risen relative to those prevailing in foreign financial centers. Thus, the interest that has to be paid on sterilization bonds denominated in domestic currency exceeds the income earned on US treasuries and other foreign-currency-denominated debt securities. Sterilizing capital flows essentially involves exchanging sterilization bonds for foreign assets (while leaving the money supply unchanged). The result is an adverse income or balance sheet effects for the emerging market central bank. The alternative would be to exchange the inflow of foreign exchange for cash. But this would be inflationary and could encourage unsustainable credit and real estate dynamics.

These problems have all been evident in Korea. There have been three recent periods of extensive intervention in the foreign exchange market: during the currency crisis, between 2003 and 2006, and 2008. The first episode was when the authorities were attempting to prevent the won from depreciating excessively; the Bank of Korea therefore sold dollars for won. This intervention ended when the inability of the authorities to contain the crisis led to the exhaustion of the Bank's dollar reserves (see Moon and Rhee, 2006). The second episode was essentially an attempt to prevent the won-dollar rate from appreciating excessively, against the dollar in particular, as the Korean economy recovered from the crisis and the country found itself on the receiving end of capital inflows. This time, the government sold won for dollars, incurring the kind of intervention costs described above. The third episode was prompted by mounting inflationary pressure, reflecting events in global commodity and energy markets in the spring of 2008. At this instance, the Bank of Korea bought won for dollars (intervention in the month of July was the largest ever in dollar terms) to prevent the exchange rate from depreciating excessively and thereby raising import prices.

Increasing Interest Arbitrage

It is interest differentials among Asian currencies that provide an incentive for arbitrage, inducing capital flows. It is useful to distinguish three types of arbitrage transaction. The first is covered-interest arbitrage by non-residents. Non-residents borrowed foreign currency and acquired Korean won using sell-buy swaps on the non-deliverable forward (NDF) market. They then invested their won in Korean bonds. Given the gap between the forward premium on foreign exchange and the interest differential, significant capital inflows were associated with these transactions for several years through 2004 (see Fig. 4.6). Inflows were especially massive in early 2004 due to the arbitrage opportunity created by the temporary regulation of NDF positions.[3] Capital inflows were 1.7 trillion Korean won in the month of February alone (Suh, 2005). However, the incentive for arbitrage evaporated as the Korean government eased its regulation of the NDF market.

A second and more important form of interest arbitrage was undertaken by foreign banks. When the forward premium was less than the

---

[3] The Korean government thought that rapid appreciation of the Korean won in the second half of 2003 was due to speculative selling of dollars in the won-dollar NDF market. Thus, to discourage investors' speculation and to lessen appreciation pressure on the Korean won, the government tried to limit forward purchase of US dollars by Korean banks, introducing a restriction on their net NDF positions. Domestic Korean banks were banned from increasing net-long dollar positions by NDF trades by more than 10% of their position on 14 January 2004. This restriction decreased forward premium and widened the gap between forward premium and interest differentials, providing new opportunities for arbitrage trade. Later, as the restriction was eased, the gap narrowed and arbitrage opportunities disappeared.

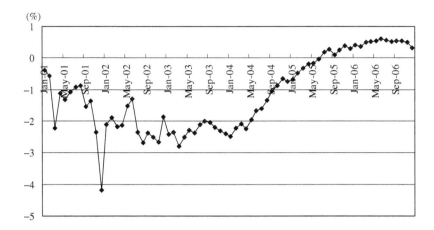

Figure 4.6. Deviations from covered interest parity.
Source: Bloomberg and Bank of Korea (http://ecos.bok.or.kr/).

interest differential, their branches and subsidiaries borrowed dollars from parent banks abroad, swapped them for won, and invested in Korean government bonds or Monetary Stabilization Bonds (see Appendix 4.1). Figure 4.7 shows the close negative correlation between interest arbitrage gains as measured by the differential between fixed won interest rates and variable Monetary Stabilization Bond rates on one hand and purchases of Korean bonds by foreign bank branches on the other. The value of Korean bonds held by foreign bank branches reached 66 trillion Korean won (approximately 70 billion US dollars) in December 2006.

Third, foreign bank branches and domestic banks undertook straight interest arbitrage transactions (see Appendix 4.2). Compared to foreign bank branches, domestic banks had to borrow at a higher cost. Moreover, because domestic banks extending foreign currency loans were exempted from the requirement that they contribute to credit guarantee funds — something that was obligatory for the issuer of an ordinary loan in domestic currency — they had a further incentive to expand their foreign currency loans.[4] This led them to lend in foreign currency, making use of

----

[4] Banks in Korea are required to make contributions at the rate of 0.25% on their outstanding domestic currency loans for credit services provided by credit guarantee funds. Such obligatory contributions have been extended to foreign currency loans since July 2007.

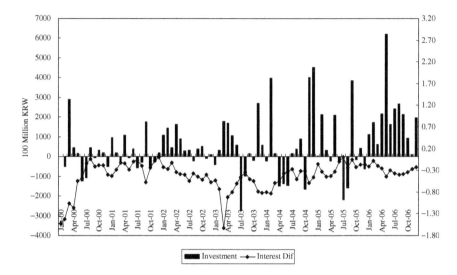

Figure 4.7. Interest arbitrage and domestic bond purchases by foreign bank branches, January 2000–December 2006.
Source: Bloomberg and Korea Securities Depository.

currency swaps. Arbitrage through foreign currency loans linked to currency swaps became possible in October 2001 when the limit on foreign currency loans was lifted. As of December 2006, the outstanding foreign currency loans by Korean banks reached $44 billion (see Fig. 4.8).

Together, these different kinds of arbitrage transactions created large short-term capital flows. These, in turn, made the stabilization of the Korean won extremely difficult.

Techniques of Foreign Exchange Market Intervention in Korea

Foreign exchange market intervention in Korea is conducted in several ways. The first is to use the Foreign Exchange Stabilization Fund established in 1967. The government issues stabilization bonds and purchases dollars. The second is to intervene in the forward market. The third is for the government to borrow from the Bank of Korea and use the funds to buy dollars. The Bank of Korea, in turn, issues Monetary Stabilization Bonds to drain the additional liquidity from the financial system, sterilizing the impact on the money stock.

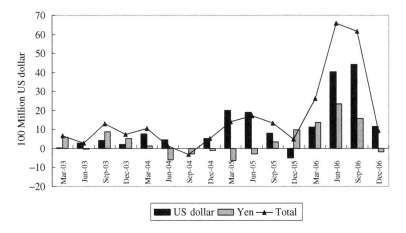

Figure 4.8. Changes in foreign currency loans of Korean banks, 2003–2006.
Source: Bank of Korea.

Table 4.2. Size of exchange stabilization fund and its performance (trillion won).

	Asset	Liability	Accumulated losses/profits
2000	14.5	15.0	−0.5
2001	13.8	14.4	−0.6
2002	18.4	20.9	−2.5
2003	31.0	33.9	−3.0
2004	38.7	54.1	−15.4
2005	49.9	68.8	−18.9
2006	54.1	80.1	−26.0
2007	64.8	91.1	−26.4

Source: National Assembly Budget Office (2008).

Table 4.2 shows the balance sheet of the Exchange Stabilization Fund. As of 2007, its liabilities reached 91 trillion won, while its assets were only 64.8 trillion won. This huge loss of 26 trillion won, the equivalent of 40 percent of assets, is essentially due to foreign exchange market intervention conducted by the Korean government since 2004. As shown in the third and fourth columns of Table 4.3, much of this loss was due to

Table 4.3. Current profits and losses by source (trillion won).

	Total profits and losses	Due to interest differentials	Due to valuation losses	Due to derivative transactions
2000	0.4	−0.4	0.9	—
2001	−0.1	−0.6	0.4	—
2002	−1.7	−0.8	−0.9	—
2003	−0.3	−1.1	0.3	0.4
2004	−12.5	−1.4	−6.5	−4.5
2005	−3.4	−1.3	−2.5	0.4
2006	−7.1	−1.1	−5.6	−0.4
2007	−0.3	−1.4	0.4	0.5
Sum	−25.2	−8.4	−13.4	−3.4

Source: National Assembly Budget Office (2008).

the excess of Korean interest rates over foreign interest rates of the sort described above.[5] The other main factor affecting the balance sheet of the Exchange Stabilization Fund was capital losses on dollar-denominated assets due to dollar depreciation.

To supplement the operations of the fund, the government carried out forward intervention in the NDF market.[6] In addition, there existed a ceiling for the issuance of the Exchange Stabilization Bonds (ESBs) and thus for the amount of Korean won that could be deployed to prevent the currency from appreciating. For example, the ceiling of 20 trillion won was already essentially binding in 2004, and further bond issuance required prior authorization by the National Assembly.[7] Resorting to the forward market was a way of circumventing this requirement.

More generally, forward market intervention was a way of camouflaging the extent of intervention and of not exciting investors who might fear declines in the prices of Korean bonds if the latter were issued excessively. These forward market operations were recorded under

[5] In addition, forward market intervention carried out by the Korean government raised the loss enormously (see below).
[6] In fact, when the Korean government had also used the forward market as a vehicle for foreign exchange intervention in the currency crisis period, it incurred serious losses, which helped to precipitate the currency crisis.
[7] In 2004, the original ceiling on ESB issuance for the year was 9 trillion won, but the limit was later raised to 20 trillion won.

Table 4.4. Reserve money, MSBs, and interest costs (trillion won).

	Reserve money	MSB outstanding	Interests paid
1999	28.4	51.5	3.8
2000	28.2	66.4	4.7
2001	32.8	79.1	4.9
2002	37.9	84.3	4.8
2003	40.7	105.5	5.0
2004	38.7	142.8	5.6
2005	43.2	155.2	6.1
2006	51.9	158.4	6.8
2007	56.4	150.3	7.5

Source: Bank of Korea.

the heading "miscellaneous income and interest to pay". But they again exposed the authorities to capital losses if the won continued to appreciate — as it in fact did. The last column of Table 4.3 shows the losses of 4.5 trillion won in 2004 and 3.4 trillion won in 2007 as a result of these forward market operations.

In addition to use of the Exchange Stabilization Fund and forward market intervention, the Korean government used money borrowed from the Bank of Korea to intervene. To absorb the increase in liquidity, the Bank of Korea sold Monetary Stabilization Bonds (MSBs). Table 4.4 shows outstanding MSBs together with the cost of stabilization. In 1999, at the outset of the post-crisis period, MSB had amounted to just 51.5 trillion won. They then began rising rapidly, reaching over 150 trillion won in 2005. Interest paid on these obligations reached 7.5 trillion won in 2007, rising up from 3.8 trillion won in 1999.

This experience shows how burdensome it became for the authorities to attempt to keep the exchange rate from moving. Yet, despite these costs, exchange-rate stabilization was never entirely abandoned as a policy objective. This is indicative of the deeply entrenched nature of the Asian growth model.

Approaches to Monetary Cooperation in East Asia

The economies of East Asia have become so interdependent that sharp movements in the exchange rates among Asian currencies can disrupt not just the operation of financial markets but also production, trade, and FDI.

This is especially the case when exchange rates appear to move in directions contrary to the fundamentals. Table 4.5 summarizes currency movements in the region. It shows that between 2000 and 2006, the yen depreciated against the dollar despite the fact that it was the United States and not Japan that was in massive current account deficit. Similarly, the won appreciated strongly against the yen despite the fact that Korea was continually running a trade deficit with Japan. These examples of seemingly perverse exchange-rate movements encourage arguments for some form of currency cooperation.[8]

However, it is increasingly difficult, as argued above, for individual countries to do anything about this given the reality of high capital mobility. This suggests a regional monetary union as an alternative solution. But, given limits on the willingness of national governments in Asia to cede sovereignty to a regional central bank (or, for that matter, to any other supranational regional institution), monetary union is at best a long-term goal.

What can be done in the interim? A more modest option would be to attempt to create an exchange-rate arrangement modeled on the European Monetary System (EMS) of the 1980s, the arrangement that was, in some

Table 4.5. Exchange rate changes vis-à-vis the US dollar, yen, won, and yuan, December 2000 to December 2006 (unit: %).

Against	US dollar	Yen	Won	Yuan
Yen	3.52	—	—	—
Won	−26.47	−29.99	—	—
Yuan	−5.66	−9.18	20.81	—
Singapore dollar	−11.43	−14.95	15.04	−5.77
Thai baht	−16.69	−20.21	9.78	−11.03
Indo. rupee	−5.99	−9.51	20.43	0.33
Mal. ringgit	−7.07	−10.59	19.40	−1.41
Phil. peso	−1.73	−5.25	27.74	3.93

Source: International Monetary Fund, *International Financial Statistics*.
Note: (+) indicates depreciation and (−) indicates appreciation.

---

[8] The mid-1990s, when the dollar appreciated against the yen, diminishing the competitiveness of many East Asian countries in the Japanese market and setting the stage for the financial crisis, is also invoked in support of this argument (see Ito *et al.*, 1998; McKinnon, 1998).

sense, the stalking horse for Europe's monetary union (see the discussion of this in Chapter 6 by De Grauwe in this volume). Here are three important decisions: the choice of parity, the width of the band, and the mechanics of foreign exchange intervention. As for the question of parities, the dominant proposal is for each currency to be stabilized against a basket of other currencies. There are two variants. The first one, advanced primarily by Japanese authors, is to make the dollar, the euro, and the yen the three components of the basket. This would stabilize emerging East Asia's currencies against one another by stabilizing them against what have been traditionally those countries' primary export markets. But this scheme does not take into account the growing economic interdependence of the economies of emerging East Asian itself — of the fact that, increasingly, they are important export markets for one another. This scheme would also place a disproportionate stabilization burden on the emerging economies themselves. Neither the United States nor the Euro area will be prepared to intervene if an emerging East Asian currency either appreciates or depreciates against the basket. Moreover, as this scheme is conventionally formulated, Japan also does not have an obligation to intervene. To be sure, pegging against a basket of extra-regional currencies is better than pegging against a single extra-Asian currency insofar as it frees emerging East Asian countries from dislocations caused by dollar-euro and dollar-yen fluctuations. But the other disadvantages of dollar pegging would remain.

A preferable alternative would be for East Asian countries to define the basket in terms of their own currencies. This is, in fact, what Europe did in the 1970s and 1980s (as described further in Chapter 6 by De Grauwe in this volume). This approach can foster cooperation on monetary and financial issues by encouraging dialog and repeated interaction. Ultimately, it can provide a basis for constructing the kind of supranational regional institutions needed to move on to a monetary union. Moreover, if the basket is really a basket (in other words, if a variety of regional currencies have significant weights), this approach can alleviate fears about the Japanese dominance of any Asian monetary arrangement.

Asian countries have, in fact, already begun to discuss the creation of such a basket. In the meeting of the ADB in Hyderabad, India in 2006, finance ministers from Korea, China, and Japan announced that they would take steps to coordinate their currencies in a way designed to ultimately produce a common regional currency similar to the euro.

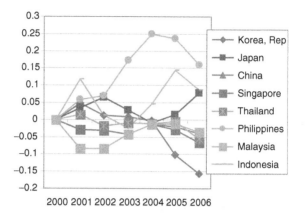

Figure 4.9. Regional currency unit rates for various Asian currencies.
Source: Updated from Moon *et al.* (2006).

They started with steps designed to lead to the creation of the so-called Regional Currency Unit (RCU). A first step will be to use the RCU as a divergence indicator in the exchange-rate coordination dialog. Moon *et al.* (2006) show how this can be done. They track a hypothetical basket currency made up of Asian currencies and construct a +/−15 percent band around it. Figure 4.9 shows that Korea was out of this band in 2006, as was the Philippines in 2004–06.

Should East Asian countries adopt a narrow band or a wide band? Given that their economies are heterogeneous, the second option seems more appropriate. Wide bands leave more room for policy independence, which will quiet fears that, in committing to this common exchange-rate arrangement, countries are compromising their sovereignty. An example of a wide-band arrangement of this sort is the basket-based target zone of Williamson (1999).

Finally, a multilateral exchange-rate system must include emergency liquidity facilities (Moon *et al.*, 2000). The official reserve holdings that a weak-currency country can mobilize on its own to finance intervention in the foreign exchange market may not suffice, given the liquidity of financial markets. Swap lines and credits that allow for the pooling of reserves are therefore needed for a sturdy defense. In the EMS, emergency liquidity was provided through the Very Short-Term Financing Facility (VSTFF), without which the system would have quickly failed. Under the VSTFF, the central banks of strong currencies were obliged to provide unlimited amounts of their own currencies to defend the existing exchange-rate margin, at least in principle.[9]

In Asia, recent progress under the CMI may facilitate development of an analogous system for providing emergency liquidity. Of course, the CMI, as currently constituted, is limited in the sense that it provides East Asian countries a swap arrangement only between their national currencies and the US dollar. Moreover, the amounts to be swapped are strictly limited. Together, these facts mean that participating central banks cannot rely on their power to print money to provide intervention currencies; intervention is still limited by the availability of reserves. The CMI will have to be elaborated further before it can provide the basis for a basket-based Asian monetary system analogous to the EMS.

Conclusion

Growing economic and financial interdependence in East Asia heightens the urgency that policymakers in the region attach to the maintenance of exchange-rate stability. At the same time, the removal of capital controls and the growth of international financial markets expose their economies and financial systems to large short-term capital flows, making unilateral exchange-rate stabilization difficult if not impossible. The dilemma is most clearly evident in the case of China, where expectations that the renminbi will be revalued have led to large anticipatory capital inflows and forced the authorities to undertake costly efforts to limit appreciation of the exchange rate. Now that Chinese interest rates exceed those in the major foreign financial centers, this intervention has become increasingly costly (see the discussion in Chapter 7 by Yu in this volume). The uncomfortable conclusion is that not even a large country like China with nearly $2 trillion of foreign exchange reserves can stabilize its exchange rate unilaterally for an indefinite period. And what is true of China is true more generally.

Resolving this dilemma requires action on the part of East Asia to establish some form of collective exchange-rate arrangement, starting presumably a set of basket-based currency pegs. Whether they will succeed

---

[9] The practice may be more complicated; see the discussion in Eichengreen's chapter in this volume.

is yet to be seen. Active policy dialog to coordinate economic and monetary policies and to achieve greater convergence in macroeconomic conditions are the logical next steps in moving down this road.

Appendix 4.1: Interest Arbitrage by the Branches of Foreign Banks in Korea Effected through Currency Swaps

In this transaction, branches of foreign banks borrow US dollars from parent banks abroad at LIBOR and convert them into Korean won through cross-currency rate swap (CRS) "receive transactions" (receiving variable US dollar interest while paying fixed Korean won interest). Then, they purchase MSB issued by the Bank of Korea. The revenue (A) of the foreign bank will be the sum of the yield rate on a MSB and the CRS variable US dollar rate (LIBOR), while its cost (B) will be the sum of the CRS fixed won rate and the US dollar borrowing rate. Figure 4A.1 shows the structure of this arbitrage transaction. Assuming that the fixed Korean won swap rate is 4.34 percent, the yield of a MSB is 4.68 percent, and the borrowing rate of US dollars from their parent banks is LIBOR, net income of the foreign bank branches will be A − B = 0.34%.

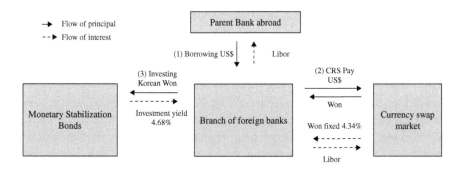

Revenue	MSB (4.68%) + CRS variable dollar rate (LIBOR)
Cost	CRS fixed won rate (4.34%) + Dollar borrowing rate (LIBOR)
Arbitrage gain	0.34%

Figure 4A.1. Arbitrage transaction by foreign bank branches.
Source: Shin *et al.* (2006).

Appendix 4.2: Interest Arbitrage by Korean Banks Effected Through Foreign Currency Loans Linked to Currency Swap Transactions

Alternatively, domestic banks could borrow US dollars abroad and lend it to domestic firms. Then, they make a currency swap "receive transaction" (receiving fixed won interest against paying variable dollar interest) with domestic firms. This swap leads domestic firms to consider the effect of foreign currency loan the same as that of Korean won loan. At the same time, domestic banks make another swap "pay transaction" (paying fixed won interest while receiving variable dollar interest) in currency swap markets. Assume that the US dollar borrowing rate abroad is LIBOR + 0.15 percent, the dollar loan rate by domestic banks is LIBOR + 0.40 percent, and the CRS rate between domestic banks and firms (Korean won fixed rate against LIBOR) is 5.80 percent, while the currency swap rate in the swap market (Korean won fixed rate against LIBOR) is 4.23 percent. Then, the revenue (A)

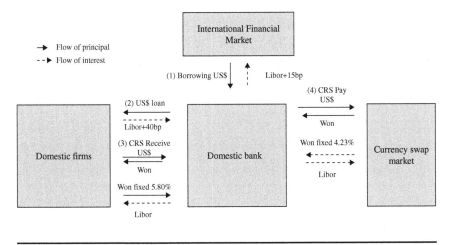

Revenue	US dollar loan rate (LIBOR + 0.40%) + CRS interest differential (5.80% − 4.23%)
Cost	Dollar borrowing rate (LIBOR + 0.15%)
Arbitrage gain	1.82%

Figure 4A.2. Arbitrage transaction by Korean banks.
Source: Shin *et al.* (2006).

would be the US dollar loan rate (LIBOR + 0.40 percent) plus the CRS interest differential (5.80% − 4.23%), while the cost (B) would be the US dollar borrowing rate (LIBOR + 0.15 percent). Net income would be A − B = 1.82%. Figure 4A.2 represents such an arbitrage transaction.

CHAPTER 5

An Asian Currency Unit for Regional Exchange-Rate Policy Coordination

Masahiro Kawai

Introduction

ASEAN+3 finance ministers have been pursuing regional financial co-operation since the outbreak of the Asian financial crisis of 1997–98. Reflecting lessons learned from the crisis, the aim has been to strengthen and integrate national financial markets and to establish regional self-help mechanisms for crisis prevention and management. Their efforts have focused on regional economic surveillance (i.e., the Economic Review and Policy Dialogue (ERPD)), a regional short-term liquidity arrangement (i.e., the Chiang Mai Initiative (CMI)), and local currency bond market development (i.e., the Asian Bond Markets Initiative (ABMI)). Asian central bank governors, participating in the Executives' Meeting of East Asia-Pacific Central Banks (EMEAP), have also made efforts to improve their policy dialog and promote local currency bond markets, e.g., through Asian Bond Funds (ABF).

While there has been substantial progress in all these areas, little progress has been made in monetary and exchange-rate policy coordination. Given the high and rising degree of economic interdependence through market-driven trade, investment, and financial activity, East Asian economies have found it increasingly important to maintain relatively stable intraregional exchange rates while allowing currency flexibility against the US dollar. A first, modest step in this direction could be the creation of an Asian Currency Unit (ACU), which could begin simply as an appropriately weighted index of East Asian currencies for the purpose of monitoring the collective movement of regional currencies against key external currencies — such as the US dollar and the euro — and each component currency's movement relative to the ACU regional benchmark. Such an index could also be used by markets for varied purposes and, once certain conditions are met in the future, the ACU could be used by the region's authorities for purposes of official accounting units, monetary transactions, and exchange-rate policy coordination. This possibility was pursued by the ASEAN+3 Research Group during 2006–08. However, no official decision has been made as to the creation of an ACU or its index.

This chapter explains the objectives of creating such a currency unit, clarifies some technical issues to be resolved in constructing it, provides the economic logic of the unit, offers preliminary currency weights for unit construction, and explores its potential role for economic surveillance and future exchange-rate policy coordination in East Asia. This chapter demonstrates how the ACU, once introduced and made operative, can become an important tool in regional economic surveillance and policy dialog, help deepen Asian financial markets — particularly for local currency-denominated bonds — and contribute to further monetary and financial cooperation. One of the critical impediments to the creation of the unit is the absence of agreements on currency weights, particularly among the so-called "plus-three" countries — China, Japan, and Korea. This chapter argues that the ongoing CMI multilateralization process is a useful catalyst for such an agreement as it involves agreements on individual countries' contributions to a new, multilateral CMI.

Objectives of Creating an ACU

The creation of an ACU was first proposed by Kuroda and Kawai (2002).[1] An ACU can be useful in three ways:

- as a statistical indicator summarizing the collective movement of Asian currencies;
- as a currency basket used by the market and
- as an official unit for monetary and exchange-rate policy coordination.

---

[1] See also Kawai and Takagi (2005b) as well as Mori *et al.* (2002). Kawai (2006) explains early thought. Other useful references include Watanabe and Ogura (2006), Chai and Yoon (2007), and Moon and Rhee (2007).

Objectives on ACU

First, the immediate objective of creating an ACU is to use it as one of the tools for monitoring foreign exchange market conditions. It represents the collective movement of regional currencies against key external currencies, such as the US dollar, the euro, and the British pound. Also, as a regional benchmark, an ACU can help gauge the degree of divergence of each component currency. A detailed analysis of divergence indicators offers valuable information for identifying idiosyncratic problems in a particular currency's market and in helping pursue appropriate macroeconomic policies to eliminate vulnerabilities that adversely affect the exchange rate.[2] In this sense, the ACU is nothing more than a statistical indicator that is useful for regional policy dialog and national policymaking, the one that does not require automatic policy changes or market interventions. Thus, it may be more appropriate to call the currency unit an ACU index.

Second, the ACU index, if constructed in a market-friendly way, can be useful for economic and financial transactions. Commercial banks could accept ACU deposits and make ACU loans. Capital markets may develop ACU-denominated bonds. Asian governments, or any other creditworthy government in the world could issue sovereign or quasi-sovereign bonds in ACU; private corporations of any nationality could issue corporate bonds in ACU; and pension, provident, and mutual funds and other institutional investors could invest in ACU-denominated bonds.[3] Both Asian and non-Asian central banks could hold part of their foreign exchange reserves in ACU. Asia's futures exchanges may develop and list new, tradable instruments such as ACU futures, which can provide hedging devices for traders — even in the absence of active onshore derivatives markets for some highly regulated currencies. Looking beyond the financial markets, exporters and importers may denominate cross-border trade in ACU.

---

[2] For example, the rapid depreciation of the Indonesian rupiah in August 2005 relative to other East Asian currencies — called the "mini-currency crisis" — signaled that the economy required monetary tightening to contain inflation and strong fiscal measures to reduce the budget deficit. Other examples include the recent carry trades that apparently caused a weak yen and a strong Korean won from 2005 to mid-2007, and the Thai baht appreciation and the subsequent, failed attempt to control capital inflows in December 2006.

[3] See Ito and Park (2004) and Dammers and McCauley (2006) for the case for developing basket currency bonds.

Third, in the future, and at a more advanced stage of its development, the ACU could play a significantly important official role, similar to that played by the European Currency Unit (ECU) within the European Monetary System (EMS) during the 1980s and 1990s (Box 1). Following the European path, East Asian authorities may decide in the years to come to stabilize their exchange rates against the ACU basket — as initially intended under the Exchange-Rate Mechanism (ERM) in Europe. Official ACUs may be created by a regional reserve pooling institution similar to the European Monetary Cooperation Fund (EMCF), and Asian central banks may be authorized to use official ACUs to settle balances with other central banks. Alternatively, an ACU could be allowed to function as a regional "parallel currency," as part of a market-driven approach to East Asian monetary integration as suggested by Eichengreen (2006). The ACU as a parallel currency would compete against other national currencies in the region for use as a unit of account, medium of exchange, and store of value.

Box 1: A Brief Timeline of European Exchange-Rate Policy Coordination

- After several years of financial instability following the Nixon shock in 1971, European countries exited the Bretton Woods dollar-peg regime and moved to a floating-rate regime against the US dollar. But for fear of volatile exchange rates among themselves, several European countries embarked on the "Snake" to maintain intraregional exchange-rate stability.
- Members of the European Community (EC) defined the European Unit of Account (EUA) as a basket of EC-9 currencies in 1975 with its initial value set equal to the June 1974 value of 1 SDR. The EUA was used as part of a policy of standardizing the accounting units for calculating the values of payments and receivables into and out of the accounts in the various spheres of Community activity — such as the European Development Fund (1975), the European Investment Bank (1975), the European Coal and Steel Community (1976), and the Community general budget (1978). Currency weights of EUA were determined by

(Continued)

Box 1: (*Continued*)

member states' GNP, intracommunity trade, and commitments to the short-term monetary support (STMS) mechanism that had been introduced since February 1970.

- In 1979, European countries launched the EMS to establish a formal, more systematic mechanism for achieving intraregional exchange-rate stability. For this purpose, they introduced: (i) the ERM that specified both a band for a central parity and rules for currency market intervention and monetary policy adjustment; (ii) the very short-term financing facility (VSTFF) that enabled central banks to intervene in currency markets without disruptions and (iii) the ECU, replacing the EUA, as a common unit of account for intraregional exchange-rate stabilization. European central banks attempted to stabilize intraregional exchange rates within a narrow fluctuation band using the ECU as a tool for defining central parities.
- While European currencies remained free to fluctuate against the US dollar, whenever the value of participating currencies in the ERM reached the upper or lower limit of the fluctuation band, central banks were obliged to intervene in the currency market to keep the value within band limits. However, in practice, the German deutschemark became the *de facto* anchor currency for exchange market interventions for non-German central banks and the Bundesbank pursued a relatively autonomous monetary policy. Hence, the symmetrically designed ERM actually operated asymmetrically with the deutschemark functioning as the *de facto* key currency in Europe.
- The composition of the ECU changed twice after its introduction, but was frozen in November 1993, when the Treaty on European Union (the Maastricht Treaty) came into effect. The freeze was irrevocable until the beginning of the final stage of Economic and Monetary Union (EMU), while the actual currency weights fluctuated due to changes in market exchange rates.
- The ECU became the basis for the newly introduced European single currency, the euro, at the start of the European Monetary Union in January 1999. The euro became the sole currency and legal tender replacing the national currencies of participating member EMU states in January 2002.

ECU and ACU

Against the backdrop of the evolution of monetary cooperation in Europe and the creation of the euro, it is crucial to emphasize the significant difference between the ECU and the proposed ACU index. The ECU was an official common unit of account introduced in March 1979 as part of the EMS. It replaced the EUA, which had been adopted by the European Community (EC; now EU). Backed by a substantial reserve fund, the EMCF, the ECU played a fundamental role in the EMS. Both official and private ECUs were created. The official ECU was provided by the EMCF to the member central banks in exchange for three-month swaps of 20% of their holdings of gold and US dollar reserves. Through this process, official ECUs were added to the reserves of participating central banks. In addition to being a common accounting unit for the EC and its various agencies — including the EMCF — the official ECU was used as a means of settling balances among member central banks, which intervened in foreign exchange markets. It was also designed to function as an indicator of a member currency's divergence from the average value of EMS currencies.

In contrast, the proposed ACU index is merely an informal statistical indicator rather than an official currency unit — at least until authorities decide otherwise. Initially, ACU index movements, and each component currency's divergence from it, require neither an automatic policy response nor any obligation for exchange market intervention. In this sense, an ACU index simply offers additional information in helping monitor currency market developments. Once Asian monetary authorities decide to pursue monetary and exchange-rate policy coordination (either along the line of the European experience or by using a different approach), however, the ACU may gain official — or even legal tender — status. Of course, it will take years or even decades before such a decision is made (if at all) given the various impediments to the evolution of Asian monetary integration.[4]

---

[4] For two or more countries to adopt and successfully maintain a common monetary and exchange-rate policy, it is necessary to achieve: (i) optimum currency area (OCA) conditions including sufficient economic integration — for goods, services, capital, and labor markets; (ii) economic and structural convergence across economies in terms of per capita incomes, market infrastructure and institutions, financial market development and openness, and monetary policy practices and (iii) political commitment to monetary integration. Though East Asia has already achieved significant economic integration through trade and foreign direct investment (FDI), the region is still weak in the other aspects. Anderson (2006) pointed out the importance of economic convergence in the ratios of purchasing power parity (PPP) to market exchange rates and argued that currently Asian economies have a significantly larger variation in these ratios than do the 12 countries of the Euro area.

Nonetheless, it is useful to have the perspective that the role of an ACU — though limited initially — can be expanded as progress is made toward greater exchange-rate policy coordination.

Constructing an ACU Index — Technical Issues

In constructing a weighted index of Asian currencies, or an ACU, several technical issues need to be addressed[5]:

- choice of fixed shares vs. fixed units of component currencies in the basket;
- choice of economic variables and indicators used to calculate currency weights/units;
- coverage of currencies included in the basket and
- frequency of periodic revisions of currency shares/units.

First, a decision must be made whether to use fixed currency shares or fixed currency units in constructing an ACU. Given ECU experience, constructing the ACU as fixed units of component currencies is more suitable. The fixed units formula, as opposed to the fixed shares formula, can produce a smooth change in the ACU index when revising the number of each currency unit, adding a new currency to the basket, or eliminating an incumbent currency from the basket. Under the fixed units formula, effective weights of individual currencies in the basket fluctuate as their exchange rates change.

Second, a decision has to be made as to what economic variables should be used in calculating the appropriate numbers of currency units in a basket. How to choose these economic variables depends on the ultimate objective for constructing the currency basket. In general, economic size matters in any currency basket as it represents the relative importance of a country in the global and regional economies. If the objective is to measure relative international price competitiveness of Asian economies against the rest of the world or among Asian economies, then a measure of trade activity will be the most important indicator. If the objective is to measure the relative importance of cross-border financial and capital transactions, then such variables as the size of international financial transactions and a measure of overall capital account convertibility are important factors to consider.

---

[5] See Girardin and Steinherr (2008) for such technical discussions.

As the objective is a combination of all of these, I suggest three types of variables for consideration: (i) the size of the economy; (ii) the size of foreign trade and (iii) the size of cross-border capital account transactions. US dollar-based gross domestic product (GDP) converted at market exchange rates — rather than at PPP — is the best proxy for economic size of an economy, as it captures the current monetary value of overall national economic activity — rather than measuring a country's standard of living. Total trade value — exports plus imports — is an appropriate measure of trade activity, though a decision has to be made on the choice between total trade with the rest of the world and total trade with regional partners.[6] In the case of ECU, intraregional trade was used as one of three "economic" criteria for constructing the basket — the other two being GDP and the quota of the individual member countries in the short-term support facility (Girardin and Steinherr, 2008). Total volume of international financial transactions — like the value of international debt securities issued by residents — is a good proxy for cross-border capital account transactions.[7] These three economic variables can be used in combination in constructing an ACU index.

Third, the question of which currencies to include in an ACU index must be addressed. Currency baskets of various subregional groups within Asia — such as East Asia, South Asia, Central Asia, and Oceania — may be considered separately. Including all Asian currencies in a single basket would be too complex and may not mean much because of the extreme diversity of economies. The most promising group thus far is a subset of East Asia — ASEAN+3 — as its members have actively pursued monetary and financial cooperation since the outbreak of the Asian financial crisis.[8] Following the recent launch of the East Asia Summit in December 2005, an ACU index including the currencies of India, Australia,

---

[6] Other current account transactions such as remittances and investment income flows may also be considered.

[7] Another useful measure could be the degree of capital account openness as shown by the IMF's *Annual Report on Exchange Arrangements and Exchange Restrictions*, (2007).

[8] ASEAN+3 includes the 10 ASEAN member countries (Brunei, Cambodia, Indonesia, Lao PDR, Malaysia, Myanmar, the Philippines, Singapore, Thailand, and Vietnam) plus China, Japan, and Korea. Hong Kong may be added to this group as it is also an active participant of ASEAN+3 finance and central bank deputies' processes and a key member of the Executives' Meeting of East Asia Pacific Central Banks (EMEAP). EMEAP includes Australia, China, Hong Kong, Indonesia, Japan, Korea, Malaysia, New Zealand, the Philippines, Singapore, and Thailand.

and New Zealand — in addition to those of ASEAN+3 — might also be considered (Gupta and Palit, 2008). There can be various combinations of currency coverage, and new currencies may be added to any initial currency basket if deemed appropriate. The formula should thus maintain an open-ended currency composition system.

Fourth, a decision must be made on the frequency of periodical revisions of assigned currency units in the basket. This decision is important not only for the authorities of component currencies, but also especially for markets, as changes in weighting will affect interest rates calculated on the different currency components of the basket and, hence, the value of the various financial instruments denominated in ACU. It is therefore important to set transparent rules for periodic revisions of units to allow financial market analysts to easily calculate basket interest rates. In the case of ECU, such revisions were made once every five years after its introduction in 1979, but the currency composition was frozen in November 1993. Given the dynamic pace of transformation of many East Asian economies, the numbers of individual currency units could be revised as often as every two to three years.

ECU Weights

The weights of the ECU were determined by participating countries' GDP, intracommunity trade, and commitments to the EMS financial support mechanism; they were at the same time "politically agreed averages" rather than mechanical weighted averages. As a result, the weight of the German deutschemark was intentionally limited below one-third. Table 5.1 summarizes the composition of the EUA and ECU baskets at different times during the existence of the two currency baskets. The EUA — the precursor of the ECU — was defined as a basket of EC-9 currencies in 1975, and its currency weights shown in the table are calculated by using 1975 exchange rates. The ECU was introduced in 1979 as the same basket as the EUA with 9 currencies, and eventually grew to a basket of 12 currencies. ECU currency composition was adjusted twice in 1984 and 1989, and was made permanently fixed in 1993.

Table 5.1 shows that currency weights of the EUA ranged from 0.3% to 27.3% and those of the ECU ranged from 0.3% to 33.0%. The maximum weights assigned to the German mark never exceeded 33%, while the lowest weights assigned to the Luxembourg franc were as low as 0.3%.

Table 5.1. Composition of EUA and ECU basket, 1975 and 1979–1999.

Currencies	EUA 1975		13 March 1979–16 Sept. 1984		17 Sept. 1984–21 Sept. 1989		21 Sept. 1989–31 Dec. 1999	
	Currency value	Weight (%)	Currency value	Weight (%)	Currency value	Weight (%)	Currency value	Weight (%)
German dm	0.828	27.3	0.828	32.98	0.719	32.08	0.6242	31.92
French franc	1.150	19.5	1.150	19.83	1.310	19.06	1.332	20.31
British pound	0.0885	17.5	0.0885	13.34	0.0878	14.98	0.08784	12.45
Dutch guilder	0.286	9.0	0.286	10.51	0.256	10.13	0.2198	9.87
Belgian franc	3.66	7.9	3.66	9.28	3.85	8.57	3.301	8.18
Italian lira	109.0	14.0	109.0	9.49	140.0	9.98	151.8	7.84
Spanish peseta	—	—	—	—	—	—	6.885	4.14
Danish krone	0.217	3.0	0.217	3.06	0.219	2.69	0.1976	2.65
Irish punt	0.00759	1.5	0.00759	1.15	0.00871	1.20	0.008552	1.09
Portuguese escudo	—	—	—	—	—	—	1.393	0.70
Greek drachma	—	—	—	—	1.15	1.31	1.44	0.44
Luxembourg franc	0.14	0.3	0.14	0.36	*	*	0.13	0.32
Total	—	100.0	—	100.00	—	100.00	—	100.00

Source: Girardin and Steinherr (2008).

Notes: (a) As the Belgian and Luxembourg francs were in a currency union in the first two periods, the combined ECU basket values are shown only for the Belgian franc.

(b) Weights are evaluated at the central parities on 13 March 1979 and 17 September 1984, and at the prevailing exchange rates on 31 December 1998, respectively.

Existing Currency Baskets

Let us examine presently existing currency basket indexes in light of the ACU index to be constructed. We review currency weights used by the US Federal Reserve (FRB), the European Central Bank (ECB), and the Bank of England (BOE) in defining their nominal effective exchange rates (NEERs) as well as those used by market participants in defining various baskets of bonds. Table 5.2 presents a summary of several currency basket weights which are adjusted so that the sum of individual ASEAN+3 currency weights equals 100%. It also includes several other emerging Asian economies (Hong Kong, Macau, Taipei, China, and India), and Australia and New Zealand for comparison.

The central banks construct NEERs using bilateral trade (export and import) relationships as weights. In the case of the FRB, ASEAN+3 accounts for 32.7% of the global US dollar NEER, while in the case of the ECB and the BOE it accounts for only 22% and 11.6% of their global NEERs, respectively. In these indexes, Japan and China naturally account for the largest weights at 27–39% of the ASEAN+3 total; followed by Korea, Hong Kong, Taipei, China, and Singapore. JPMorgan also calculates the Bloomberg–JPMorgan Asia Currency Index (ADXY) as a measure of aggregate emerging Asian currency movements (i.e., excluding the Japanese yen), using East Asia's (but including India) trade weights with non-regional economies. In ADXY, the pattern of important currency weights is basically the same as those for central bank NEERs. The Asian Monetary Unit (AMU) constructed by Japan's Research Institute of Economy, Trade and Industry (RIETI) uses trade volume and PPP-based GDP to determine currency weights. As a result, the weight assigned to China is the largest, followed by Japan, Korea, and Singapore.[9]

Several regional bond indexes have been constructed by the private sector. These include: (i) the Asian US Dollar Bond Index (ADBI) calculated by HSBC; (ii) the Asia Credit Index (JACI) provided by JPMorgan; (iii) Emerging Local Markets Index Plus (ELMI+) calculated by JPMorgan and (iv) the iBoxx Pan-Asia Index, developed by the International Index Company Limited for the Asian Bond Fund (ABF) under the EMEAP initiative. In these measures, currency weights vary across indexes, but large weights tend to be assigned to emerging economy

---

[9] See Ogawa and Shimizu (2005) and Research Institute of Economy, Trade and Industry (2006) for AMU indexes.

Table 5.2. Summary of various currency basket weights.

Currencies	Central bank NEER			Currency index		Bond market index				
	FRB	ECB	BOE	BLBG-JPM ADXY	RIET-IAMU	HSBC ADBI	JPMorgan JACI	JPMorgan ELMI+	ABF iBoxx
Chinese yuan	38.5	26.9	27.6	33.8	34.8	15.0	9.6	9.4	13.8
Japanese yen	28.9	38.7	38.8	—	27.8	—	—	—	—
Korean won	11.7	12.4	10.3	25.1	9.8	45.2	30.7	10.2	25.3
Brunei dollar	—	—	—	—	0.4	—	—	—	—
Cambodian kiep	—	—	—	—	0.2	—	—	—	—
Indonesian rupiah	2.5	3.2	—	5.0	5.1	1.9	7.2	10.4	7.3
Lao PDR kip	—	—	—	—	0.1	—	—	—	—
Malaysian ringgit	6.1	5.0	6.0	8.9	5.3	19.4	15.3	—	13.1
Myanmarese kyat	—	—	—	—	0.4	—	—	—	—
Philippines peso	2.4	2.4	—	3.8	2.9	13.0	20.5	9.6	6.1
Singaporean dollar	5.9	7.0	11.2	14.8	6.4	2.8	13.8	50.1	22.3
Thai baht	4.1	4.5	6.0	8.7	5.1	2.8	2.1	10.3	12.1
Vietnamese dong	—	—	—	—	1.8	—	0.8	—	—
ASEAN+3 currencies	100.0	100.0	100.0	100.0	100.0	100.0	100.0	100.0	100.0

(Continued)

Table 5.2. (*Continued*)

Currencies	Central bank NEER			Currency index		Bond market index			
	FRB	ECB	BOE	BLBG-JPM ADXY	RIET-IAMU	HSBC ADBI	JPMorgan JACI	JPMorgan ELMI+	ABF iBoxx
Hong Kong dollar	5.9	8.3	14.7	15.8	—	17.0	25.4	47.6	22.4
Macau dollar	—	—	—	—	—	—	0.4	—	—
New Taiwan dollar	7.9	10.4	7.8	15.4	—	—	1.2	9.6	—
Indian rupee	3.3	5.8	11.2	7.2	—	—	3.3	9.4	—
Australian dollar	3.5	3.2	11.2	—	—	—	—	—	—
New Zealand dollar	—	0.5	—	—	—	—	—	—	—

Source: Various websites.

Notes: FRB = US Federal Reserve Board's NEER (nominal effective exchange rate); ECB = European Central Bank's NEER; BOE = Bank of England's NEER; BLBG-JPM ADXY = Bloomberg-JPMorgan Asia Currency Index (currency basket); RIETI AMU = Research Institute of Economy, Trade and Industry's Asian Monetary Unit (currency basket); HSBC ADBI = HSBC's Asian USD Bond Index (USD-denominated fixed-rate straight bonds); JACI = JPMorgan Asia Credit Index (USD-denominated bonds); ELMI+ = JPMorgan Emerging Local Markets Index Plus (local currency-denominated money market instruments); ABF iBoxx = Asian Bond Fund iBoxx Pan-Asia Index (local currency-denominated bonds).

currencies like the Korean won, the Hong Kong dollar, and the Singapore dollar, while smaller weights are assigned to the Chinese yuan despite the country's large economic size. The reason is that in bond market indexes, factors like market size, liquidity, and openness are taken into account, which make currency weights of economies with developed bond markets higher and those with less developed markets lower (Box 2).

Box 2: ABF iBoxx Pan-Asia Index

- The ABF iBoxx Pan-Asia Index calculates the value of a bond fund investing in local currency government and quasi-government bonds in eight emerging East Asian markets. As the fund covers a variety of bond markets, a simple weighting by market capitalization would distort the index in favor of large markets such as the PRC and Korea and reduce the weight for smaller, but more developed, more liquid, and accessible markets such as Hong Kong and Singapore. Therefore, the weight of each economy starts from an equal weighting baseline and is then adjusted by four factors — local bond market size (20%), turnover ratio (20%), sovereign local debt rating (20%), and market openness (40%).

- The ABF iBoxx Pan-Asia Index uses the following methodology in order to measure the four factors:

  (i)   Local bond market size (S) is based on data from the Bank for International Settlements (BIS) where available, or on a consolidated average poll of the iBoxx Asian Index Committee;

  (ii) Turnover ratio (T), considered as a proxy for liquidity, is obtained as a ratio of total transaction size to market capitalization. Transaction size is obtained through the consolidated annualized average polled from the iBoxx Asian Index Committee;

  (iii) Sovereign local debt rating (R) is the best (highest) local currency long-term rating from Fitch, Moody's, or S&P by converting the rating into a numerical equivalent and

(Continued)

Box 2: (*Continued*)

(iv) Market openness (*O*) is a qualitative measurement of relative market openness, assessed on the basis of the legal and regulatory environment, the fiscal situation, market infrastructure, and back-office infrastructure — with economies being grouped into three categories: highly open (Hong Kong and Singapore); generally open (Indonesia, Korea, Malaysia, the Philippines, and Thailand); and relatively less open (China).

• Each economy's weight is calculated as the sum of the baseline weight (1/8) plus an adjustment factor that reflects the above for factors with a given set of weights:

$$W_i = (1/8) + AF_i = (1/8) + 0.2\,S_i + 0.2\,T_i + 0.2\,R_i + 0.4\,O_i$$

• A technical committee and an oversight committee review the market allocations annually. The ABF iBoxx index is rebalanced monthly.

Preliminary ACU Index

The existing currency baskets suggest that depending on the objective of creating such baskets the currency weights can vary considerably. To construct an ACU in the current East Asian context, it is crucial to ensure that the basket is effective in: (a) summarizing the collective movement of ASEAN+3 currencies, (b) encouraging the market to develop ACU-denominated financial products — such as bonds — and (c) guiding monetary and exchange-rate policy coordination in the future. For this purpose, the index should clearly reflect individual participating countries' economic size and cross-border activities in the current and capital accounts. From this perspective, an ACU index should be constructed by selecting such economic variables as GDP at market exchange rates, cross-border trade volume, and cross-border financial transactions. Once the ACU is constructed, effective currency weights can be easily altered, a new currency can be added, and any component currency can be eliminated without causing discontinuous shifts in the basket value.

Table 5.3 summarizes preliminary information on several alternative measures of currency weights based on GDP, trade volume, and capital account transactions. Gross domestic product is measured at market exchange rates. Trade volume has two options: one based on total trade volume and the other based on intraregional trade volume. Capital account transactions also have two options: one based on international debt securities (IDS) issued by residents and the other based on measures of capital controls reported by the International Monetary Fund (IMF).

Several averages of these factors are shown in the last columns of Table 5.3 as preliminary weights assigned to each currency in constructing an ACU index. In contrast to RIETI's AMU computation where PPP-based GDP was used rather than market exchange rate-based GDP, Japan has the largest weight, followed by China, Korea, and Singapore. Our preliminary weights are in the range of 32–37% for Japan, 19–23% for China, 9–15% for Korea, 8–10% for Singapore, and 24–39% for ASEAN as a group (including Singapore). Japan's weight is the largest because of its largest size of GDP based on market exchange rates, its second largest size of trade volume, and its highest degree of capital account openness. China's weight is the second largest because of its largest trade volume and its second largest GDP size despite its relatively closed capital account. Over time, China's weight is expected to grow as its nominal GDP and trade volume will rise rapidly and its capital account will become increasingly open. On the other hand, Japan's weight is expected to decline over time as many other East Asian economies will continue to grow faster than Japan, and their capital account openness will catch up with Japan's.

Economic Logic of Introducing an ACU

If one of the ultimate objectives of Asian monetary and financial cooperation is the promotion of regional monetary integration and the eventual creation of a monetary union, why is an Asian currency basket needed? We argue that an ACU is a useful first step towards monetary integration as it nurtures conditions for stable exchange rates among the region's currencies.

There are two ways to establish a stable intraregional exchange-rate relationship. One is for each economy to stabilize the exchange rate

Table 5.3. Preliminary currency weights in an ACU for ASEAN+3 countries (%).

| Currencies | Nominal GDP (at market rates) | Trade volume | | IDS | Capital account | Total average | | | |
| | | Total | Intra-regional | | Capital control | | | | |
	A	B	C	D	E	A+B+D/3	A+C+D/3	A+B+E/3	A+C+E/3
Chinese yuan	29.37	34.65	25.10	4.07	2.23	22.70	19.51	22.08	18.90
Japanese yen	48.78	24.20	22.26	39.66	24.44	37.54	36.90	32.47	31.83
Korean won	9.92	12.50	13.91	23.35	4.44	15.26	15.73	8.95	9.42
Brunei dollar	0.13	0.17	0.31	0.00	20.00	0.10	0.15	6.77	6.81
Cambodian kiep	0.08	0.13	0.17	0.00	13.33	0.07	0.08	4.51	4.53
Indonesian rupiah	4.07	3.62	6.16	2.08	4.44	3.26	4.10	4.04	4.89
Lao PDR kip	0.04	0.05	0.12	0.00	4.44	0.03	0.06	1.51	1.53
Malaysian ringgit	1.69	5.74	7.28	6.75	2.23	4.73	5.24	3.22	3.73
Myanmarese kyat	0.15	0.13	0.31	0.00	0.00	0.09	0.15	0.10	0.15
Philippines peso	1.31	2.00	3.21	8.29	2.23	3.87	4.27	1.85	2.25

(*Continued*)

Table 5.3. (*Continued*)

Currencies	Nominal GDP (at market rates)	Trade volume		Capital account		Total average			
		Total	Intra-regional	IDS	Capital control	A+B+D/3	A+C+D/3	A+B+E/3	A+C+E/3
	A	B	C	D	E				
Singaporean dollar	1.48	10.05	12.68	12.39	17.78	7.97	8.85	9.77	10.65
Thai baht	2.30	5.11	6.32	2.95	4.44	3.45	3.86	3.95	4.35
Vietnamese dong	0.68	1.65	2.17	0.46	0.00	0.73	1.10	0.78	0.96
ASEAN+3 currencies	100.00	100.00	100.00	100.00	100.00	100.00	100.00	100.00	100.00

Source: Author's calculations.

Notes: The weights are based on 2006 data. The total trade volume weight is a ratio of a country's total world trade (exports plus imports) to ASEAN+3 countries' total world trade, while the intraregional trade volume weight is the ratio of a country's total intraregional trade to ASEAN+3 countries' total intraregional trade. IDS refers to international debt securities by residence of issuer. Capital control is based on the number of capital transactions identified by the IMF as free from controls out of 13 transactions: see IMF, *Annual Report on Exchange Arrangements and Exchange Restrictions* (2007).

to a common key currency so that its exchange rates against other regional currencies become more or less stable. The other is for regional economies to adopt collective policymaking based on certain rules — such as the "Snake" and the ERM adopted by Europe in the 1970s through the 1990s. As economic, particularly structural, convergence is not sufficiently achieved among East Asian economies and their political relationships are not mature enough to initiate a tightly coordinated exchange-rate arrangement, it is more realistic to select a major currency — like the US dollar, the euro, the yen, or the yuan — or a basket of global or regional currencies as exchange rate anchor for each country's exchange-rate policymaking. Here, we argue that there is a strong case for selecting a basket of Asian currencies, rather than a broad basket of currencies or a single East Asian currency, as an anchor for exchange-rate stabilization in the region.

Dollar, Yen, or Yuan for East Asia?

Until the Asian currency crisis of 1997, the general practice had been to peg currencies to the US dollar and, by doing so, indirectly stabilize intraregional values of East Asian currencies. But this "dollar standard system" revealed its flaws during the crisis. For example, for countries with strong economic ties with Japan — those beginning to satisfy OCA conditions — pegging their currencies to the US dollar meant volatile exchange rates against the yen due to large yen-dollar rate fluctuations. This created big financial risks in managing their economies. In addition, many East Asian economies do not satisfy OCA conditions with the United States because of structural differences and dissimilar supply shocks affecting the East Asian and US economies.[10]

Pegging currencies to the yen would therefore be more reasonable, particularly given Japan's economic weight in East Asia and its multinational corporations' networking capacity throughout the region (Kwan, 2001). Continuing economic recovery from Japan's decade-long economic stagnation may also make the yen a strong candidate to become an East Asian anchor. But the problem is that Tokyo has not grown into

---

[10] Pegging to the euro would be more problematic than pegging to the US dollar or yen due to East Asia's smaller degree of economic links with Europe.

a world-class financial center comparable to New York or London or even other major Asian financial centers like Singapore and Hong Kong, and the yen has not achieved the full internationalization necessary for it to assume the sole anchor role in the region. Because of decade-long price deflation, the Bank of Japan has not been able to normalize its monetary policy. The US dollar remains the most dominant key currency in East Asia due to the failure of the yen to rise as the region's major international currency.

Current economic trends suggest that China will surpass Japan in economic size by 2020 and the EU and the United States by 2050, barring growth disruptions arising from: (i) possible economic and financial crises, (ii) tight resource, energy, and environmental constraints, or (iii) unmanageable political and social instability. Thus, there is a strong potential for the yuan to match or even exceed the role of the US dollar, euro, or yen and become a key anchor currency in the region reflecting China's rapid pace of economic growth and its ever-rising economic influences on other East Asian economies. Considering China's rising economic dominance, Woo (2007) expects East Asia's monetary regime to become a yuan bloc by 2035.

However, there are several reasons why this may not happen at least for many decades to come. First, for the yuan to become an international currency, China must transform itself into a fully open economy with regard to trade, investment, and finance. The country must allow the yuan's international use by liberalizing cross-border capital flows and currency trading. Full liberalization of the capital account requires it to complete the transition to a market economy and to establish a sound and resilient financial sector — which could take another 10–20 years, perhaps even longer. Second, even though, in a best case scenario, China's per capita income may rise from one-third to one-fifth of that in Japan, Europe, or the United States by 2050, the question remains whether China can sufficiently eliminate poverty, reduce income and social disparities, and ensure smooth political transitions — necessary caveats for a credible international currency. Third, even if the yuan becomes an international currency, the doubt remains whether it will grow into a leading international currency that can match the US dollar, as this whole process depends on the future performance of the US economy. Unless serious difficulties confront the US economy — breaking the US dollar's "law of inertia" as the incumbent international currency — it is hard to imagine the yuan alone challenging the status quo.[11]

Anchor Currency Choice: A Case for a Currency Basket

In principle, a relatively small country's currency — the Korean won, Thai baht, or any other East Asian currency — could also be chosen as an anchor currency, but this is only a theoretical possibility as economic size matters in reality. Essentially, no single currency — be it the dollar, euro, yen, or yuan — is a good candidate as sole anchor currency for East Asia for now and at least for several decades to come. In East Asia, it makes sense for a currency basket, composed of the US dollar, euro, yen, yuan, and possibly, other regional currencies together, to fulfill the requirements for an anchor. The global key currencies — the US dollar and the euro — are still important references for East Asia, while the yen (convertible but not fully internationalized) and the yuan (inconvertible but rising rapidly) can play complementary roles. Including the yuan in the basket is a must given China's growing economic stature in East Asia — particularly from a trade or competitiveness perspective. If East Asian economies stabilized their currencies against similarly defined baskets, then they could achieve relative stability of both effective and intraregional exchange rates. Essentially, the currency basket arrangement can create a stable exchange-rate environment for the entire region.

This point can be illustrated by a hypothetical game between Japan and China over the choice of an anchor currency (Table 5.4).[12] In this

---

[11] These arguments do not preclude the possibility that the yuan begins to function as an important international currency for smaller neighboring countries — such as Lao PDR, Myanmar, and Mongolia. It is said that the yuan tends to be used and held in the northern part of Lao PDR and Myanmar and in the southern part of Mongolia. This could grow as China continues its economic growth. Still, it would take a long time before the yuan becomes a credible international currency from either a worldwide or regional perspective.

[12] This is an application of the "battle of the sexes" model, which is a two-player coordination game. An example is the situation where a couple — Kelly and Chris — needs to decide whether they want to go to the football game (Kelly's preference) or the opera (Chris' preference), both hoping to go to the same place together rather than different ones alone. See Hamada (2006) for the original application of such a game.

Table 5.4. Choice of an anchor currency in a game between Japan and China.

		China			
		US dollar	yen	yuan	Thai baht
Japan	US dollar	2, 2	0, 0	0, 0	0, 0
	yen	0, 0	3, 1	0, 0	0, 0
	yuan	0, 0	0, 0	1, 3	0, 0
	Thai baht	0, 0	0, 0	0, 0	1, 1

Note: Payoffs are indicated in each cell in the order of Japan and China.

game, if Japan and China propose different currencies as regional anchor for exchange-rate stabilization — say Japan chooses the yen and China the yuan — there is no regionally consistent exchange-rate arrangement, so each country's payoff is zero. If they choose the same currency as the region's common anchor, then they both benefit from exchange-rate stabilization, but the country whose currency is chosen as anchor may gain more, with a payoff of 3, than the country whose currency is not chosen, with a payoff of 1 (though this assumption is not crucial). If both countries choose the US dollar, the payoffs are 2 each; if both countries choose the Thai baht, the payoffs are 1 each; if they choose the yen, the payoffs are 3 for Japan and 1 for China; and if they choose the yuan, the payoffs are 1 for Japan and 3 for China. The pure-strategy Nash equilibrium is the simultaneous choice of either the US dollar, the yen, the yuan, or the baht. Within the context of ASEAN+3 — composed of 13 authorities as the game's players — at least 13 Nash equilibria will be obtained (or 14 or 15 depending on whether the US dollar and/or the euro are included in the game). A mixed strategy of these multiple equilibria may be realized by choosing a basket of all these currencies.[13]

The resulting currency basket may include both regional and non-regional currencies. The collection of regional currencies can be called the ACU. If non-regional currencies are excluded from consideration as candidates for East Asia's anchor currency, then the authorities will choose a basket comprising only regional currencies, i.e., the ACU. Essentially, an

---

[13] Some technical issues need to be resolved to find appropriate weights attached to the currencies.

ACU is useful because no single Asian currency is dominant as a key currency in the region.

Exchange-Rate Regime Choice: A Case for a Currency Basket

Another way of addressing the issue is to consider a country's choice of an exchange-rate regime given other countries' choices. Even when a currency basket system is desirable from regional perspectives, it may not be easy for any single country to move unilaterally away from the current, dominant exchange-rate regime — such as the US dollar-based arrangement — to a new regime in which the relative weight of the dollar is smaller (or zero) and that of the yen and other East Asian currencies is larger.[14] When neighboring countries stabilize their exchange rates primarily against the dominant anchor currency — such as the US dollar — there may be no incentive for any one country to unilaterally alter its exchange-rate policy. This is a classical collective action problem associated with a move to an alternative exchange-rate regime — such as a move from an external-currency peg to a currency basket arrangement. Even though such a move can be Pareto-improving, individual economies may lack the incentives to do so (Ogawa and Ito, 2002). Overcoming this problem requires coordinated action among the countries concerned.

Initially, such coordination might imply the simultaneous adoption of a similar currency basket as a nominal anchor. If the currency basket includes external currencies — such as the US dollar and the euro — the operation of the regional currency basket arrangement requires less formality and has greater flexibility than the EMS of 1979–98 because the need for a formal structure of policy coordination and surveillance is less compelling. This consideration can be important when the concerned countries lack commitments to full-fledged monetary policy coordination. However, as the countries develop such policy commitments over time — due to, say, greater economic and political convergence — they may agree on a common basket and adopt more concerted monetary and fiscal policies to ensure tighter exchange-rate stability against the basket.[15] And the nature

---

[14] Honohan and Lane (1999) emphasized the existence of strategic interdependence in the choice of exchange-rate regimes for neighboring countries that compete for exports in third markets and for FDI inflows.

[15] Williamson (1999; 2000) advocates a common currency basket.

of the currency basket may evolve into a basket of regional currencies, i.e., an ACU in East Asia. At this stage, countries must be ready to make more permanent commitments to the establishment of more formal institutions capable of supporting exchange-rate policy coordination.

Potential Role of an ACU for Regional Economic Surveillance

Regional surveillance mechanisms are instrumental to exchange-rate policy coordination. There are several mechanisms in East Asia that have been developed for such purposes, including the ASEAN+3 finance ministers' process called the ERPD and the central bank governors' process called the EMEAP. These are summarized in Box 3. The common objective of these mechanisms is to strengthen policy dialog and policymaking through information exchange, peer reviews, and recommendations for concerted action at the regional level. Policymakers monitor global and regional economic conditions, capital flows, exchange-rate movements, financial sector developments, and structural issues. With effective surveillance mechanisms in place, the region's policymakers are expected to be under peer pressure so that they are guided to pursue disciplined macroeconomic and structural policies at the national levels, which are conducive to stable external accounts and currencies.

**Box 3: ASEAN+3 Finance Ministers' Initiatives for
Regional Financial Cooperation**

- Through the ASEAN+3 ERPD process, finance ministers and their deputies meet regularly to review financial and economic issues affecting member countries. Eight members have set up "national surveillance units", or their equivalents, for economic and financial monitoring and are developing their own early warning systems. To further strengthen surveillance capacity, the Group of Experts (GOE) and the Technical Working Group on Economic and Financial Monitoring (ETWG) were launched.

(Continued)

Box 3: *(Continued)*

- Since May 2005, finance ministers have substantially strengthened the CMI through: (i) integration and enhancement of ASEAN+3 ERPD into the CMI framework (May 2005); (ii) increasing the ceiling for withdrawal without an IMF program in place from 10% to 20% of the total (May 2005); (iii) adoption of the collective decision-making procedure for CMI swap activation, as a step toward CMI multilateralization (May 2006); (iv) agreement in principle on a "self-managed reserve pooling" arrangement governed by a single contractual agreement as an appropriate form of CMI multilateralization (May 2007) and (v) agreement that the total size of a multilateral CMI should be at least US$80 billion and 80% of this total should come from the "plus-three" countries and the rest from ASEAN countries (May 2008). Total bilateral swap size reached US$84 billion as of January 2008. Currently, the ASEAN+3 finance deputies are studying the key elements of CMI multilateralization (self-managed reserve pooling), including surveillance, reserve eligibility, size of commitment, borrowing quota, activation mechanism, and contribution quota in a multilateral CMI.

- The ABMI is marshalling technical expertise and building capacity for regional bond market development. Current discussions are focusing on: (i) issuance of new securitized debt instruments; (ii) establishment of a regional credit guarantee agency to help mitigate risks through credit enhancement; (iii) exploration of possible establishment of a regional clearance and settlement system to facilitate cross-border bond transactions without facing Herstatt risk (i.e., the risk of being in a different time zone) and (iv) strengthening of regional rating agencies and harmonization of rating standards.

- The ABF initiative has been undertaken by 11 East Asian central banks under EMEAP as a measure to augment demand for local currency bonds. Following the US dollar-based ABF adopted in June 2003, the second phase (ABF-2) was launched in December 2004 to invest US$2 billion of foreign exchange reserves in local

(Continued)

Box 3: (*Continued*)

currency-denominated sovereign and quasi-sovereign bonds issued by eight EMEAP members — excluding Japan, Australia, and New Zealand. ABF-2 has two components: a Pan-Asian Bond Index Fund (PAIF) — a listed open-ended bond fund with investments in eight economies' local currency sovereign and quasi-sovereign bonds; and a Fund of Bond Funds — a two-tiered structure with a parent fund investing in eight sub-funds, each investing in local currency bonds.

One of the problems of the current regional surveillance processes, however, is that policymakers have not developed a systematic framework for monitoring exchange market developments and for assessing countries' exchange-rate policies. This has been the case despite recent policy shifts and several currency market strains. These include: the shift of the Chinese yuan regime in July 2005 from its *de facto* US dollar peg to a gradual crawling appreciation vis-à-vis the dollar; the mini crisis of the Indonesian rupiah in the summer of 2005; the rapid Thai baht appreciation that triggered capital inflow controls and sharp declines in stock prices in December 2006 and the depreciation pressure on the Vietnamese dong in the face of high and rising inflation and widening current account deficits in the spring of 2008. In addition, the region is facing the risk of financial turmoil due to the US subprime crisis, US recession, and disorderly unwinding of global payments imbalances, which could result in rapid, steep appreciation of East Asian currencies vis-à-vis the dollar.

The ACU index to be developed can serve as a useful surveillance tool for monitoring currency market developments.[16] Figure 5.1 shows trends of ACU exchange rates vis-à-vis the dollar and the euro since 1995, which are constructed using the weights reported in the second column

---

[16] However, Adams and Chow (2007) and Watanabe and Ogura (2006) argue that ACU-based divergence indicators are unlikely to be used or monitored by monetary authorities, given the ECU experience. They note that even the ECU did not attract attention as a divergence indicator in Europe. In East Asia, potential for the ACU as a divergence indicator seems large because the authorities are keen on avoiding persistent misalignment in intraregional exchange rates as well as stemming irregular currency movements and currency attack on their currency.

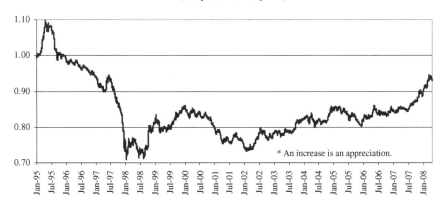

Figure 5.1. Trend of ACU vis-à-vis the USD, January 1995–April 2008.

of the total average in Table 5.3. Here, the ACU is constructed, for expository purposes, by using the simple average of columns A, C, and D in Table 5.3 as currency weights. Figures 5.2a and b shows exchange-rate movements of major ASEAN currencies and "plus-three" currencies vis-à-vis the dollar and the ACU, demonstrating sharp depreciation of crisis-affected currencies in 1997. Over time, one can observe rising deviations among East Asian exchange rates.

Figure 5.3 demonstrates the significance of the mini crisis of the Indonesian rupiah in August 2005, when investor confidence worsened, generating a sharp reversal of portfolio flows, and the stock market index slid sharply. Indonesian markets stabilized after the government announced a major cutback in fuel subsidies, which contributed to the reduction in budget deficits, and raised policy interest rates, which successfully contained inflation. Figure 5.4 demonstrates the significance of the rapid Thai baht appreciation due to hot money inflows in December 2006. Thai officials imposed controls on capital inflows, requiring 30% reserves on short-term capital inflows. When this was met by a sharp decline in equity prices in the Thai stock exchange the next day, the authorities had to announce that the inflow controls would not apply to trade, FDI, or portfolio equity, and they modified them in January 2007 to exempt hedged residential foreign currency borrowing. Subsequently, the onshore baht stabilized, though the offshore rate continued to appreciate.

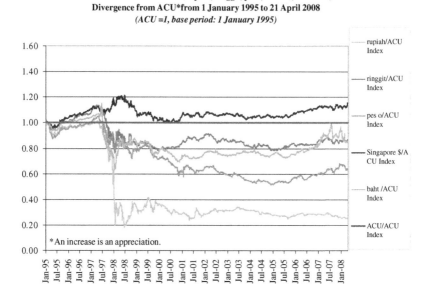

Figure 5.2a. Trend of main Asian currencies vis-à-vis the ACU, January 1995–April 2008.

Figure 5.2b. Trend of main Asian currencies vis-à-vis the ACU, January 1995–April 2008.

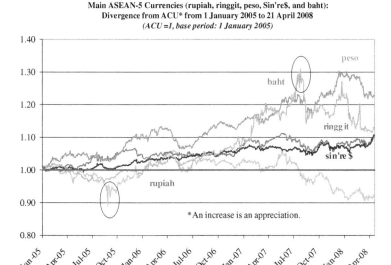

Figure 5.3. Rupiah mini crisis in August 2005 and capital controls in Thailand in December 2006 exchange rates vis-à-vis the ACU, January 2005–April 2008.

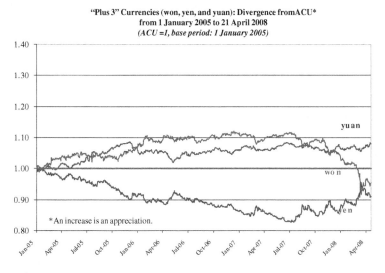

Figure 5.4. Yen, yuan, and won exchange rates vis-à-vis the ACU, January 2005–April 2008.

In this way, the ACU index and ACU divergence indicators, if properly constructed, can be useful statistical indicators to help authorities monitor regional currencies' trends. The divergence indicators are particularly informative as a market-signaling device and as a measure of a currency's performance with respect to the rest of the regional currencies, and they are easily understood by the authorities and market participants.

Potential Role of an ACU for Exchange-Rate Policy Coordination

Currently, no consensus exists, even within ASEAN+3, on a regional exchange-rate arrangement or on the potential role of an ACU. I offer here a possible scenario for the development of such an arrangement and the possible role of an ACU.[17] In this scenario, monetary and exchange-rate policy coordination deepens in a gradual, step-by-step manner, from informal policy coordination to more formal, tighter policy coordination. The first stage is to initiate informal coordination of exchange-rate regimes by moving toward greater exchange-rate flexibility. The second stage is to move to formal but loose coordination to ensure some intra-regional exchange-rate stability without rigid coordination of monetary policy. The third stage is to adopt tightly defined exchange-rate and monetary policy coordination. Each stage may be accompanied by complementary, supporting institutions to be developed in the financial and real sectors (Table 5.5).

The first stage is the introduction of informal coordination to achieve both greater exchange-rate flexibility vis-à-vis the US dollar and some intraregional exchange-rate stability by using a basket of G3 currencies (the US dollar, the euro, and the yen) or G3-plus currencies (adding emerging East Asian currencies) as a reference. This can be done by all emerging East Asian economies to adopt managed floating targeted at a G3 or G3-plus basket. The currency weights in the basket could vary across countries, at least initially. How strictly countries stabilize currencies to this

---

[17] See Kawai (2006). Although there may be other scenarios, the one proposed here is general enough to capture the substance of necessary elements of any other scenario. However, views may differ across experts and policymakers with regard to the potential role of an ACU. See also Girardin and Steinherr (2008).

Table 5.5. Steps toward exchange rate and monetary policy coordination.

Progress	Exchange-rate policy	Institutions	Trade-investment
Current state	Uncoordinated exchange-rate arrangements	CMI & ERPD; Asian Bond Markets Initiatives (ABMI)	Uncoordinated FTAs (Asian noodle bowls)
Informal coordination (exchange-rate regime coordination)	Move to greater exchange-rate flexibility vs. US dollar; A G3 or G3-plus currency basket as loose reference; ACU index for surveillance	Multilateralized CMI; Independent secretariat for CMI & ERPD among ASEAN+3 finance ministers and central bank governors	Coordination and harmonization of rules (including rules of origin) & provisions among FTAs
Loose coordination (exchange-rate policy coordination)	A G3-plus currency basket system with well-defined rules for intraregional rate stability	Asian monetary cooperation fund; Regional infrastructure for bond markets (credit guarantees, clearance, rating)	East Asian FTA (ASEAN+3 or ASEAN+6); East Asian investment area
Tight coordination (monetary policy coordination)	ACU-based system — "Asian Snake" or "Asian ERM"	Regional regulatory authority; very short-term liquidity arrangement	Asian customs union
Complete coordination	Asian monetary union	Asian central bank	Asian common market

basket could depend in each case on country conditions and preferences. National monetary authorities can maintain most of their autonomous policymaking by combining an appropriately defined monetary policy framework — including inflation targeting policy — and basket-based managed floating.

The authorities need to strengthen ongoing financial cooperation initiatives — the ERPD, CMI, ABMI, and ABF under the aegis of the ASEAN+3 finance ministers and central bank governors (Box 3).[18] One direction, which is under way in the official process, is to multilateralize the bilateral swap arrangements of the CMI and enhance regional economic surveillance under ERPD. It will be necessary to create an independent secretariat to support enhanced CMI and ERPD, where both finance ministers and central bank governors of ASEAN+3 will participate. The authorities can start using an ACU index and divergence indicators for regional exchange-rate monitoring as part of an enhanced ERPD. As China is moving towards greater exchange-rate flexibility of the yuan, the ACU index and divergence indicators can provide increasingly meaningful information. The authorities also need to make significant progress in developing local currency-denominated bond markets, particularly preparing for issuance of ACU bonds.

In the second stage, the authorities may coordinate policies to stabilize exchange rates against a common basket of G3-plus currencies (the US dollar, the euro, and the ACU) to ensure relative stability of their effective exchange rates and intraregional exchange rates. The basket stabilization policy will have to be formally defined with transparent rules for exchange-rate parity against the basket, a relatively wide exchange-rate band (like ±10%) around parity, and adjustment of both the parity and the band (as described by Williamson, 2005). The authorities would allow sufficient exchange-rate flexibility vis-à-vis the US dollar while enjoying a lesser degree of national monetary-policy autonomy. The ACU index should continue to serve as a key indicator in measuring joint movements and divergences of East Asian currencies, while policymakers may encourage the development of ACU-based financial products — such as ACU bonds.

Supporting institutional arrangements should be strengthened. A fully multilateralized CMI and a fully staffed, independent secretariat will form a regional monetary cooperation fund (an Asian Monetary Cooperation Fund (AMCF)), whose functions include: conducting regional economic

---

[18] Though central bank governors are not formally involved in the ASEAN+3 finance ministers' process, their deputies participate in the important working groups under the finance ministers. See Kuroda and Kawai (2002), Bird and Rajan (2002), Montiel (2004), Rajan and Siregar (2004), Girardin (2004), and Kawai and Houser (2008) for a review of recent initiatives undertaken by the ASEAN+3 finance ministers.

surveillance; formulating independent lending conditionality; and issuing official ACUs (see Chai and Yoon, 2007). Various regional entities will have been established to support the development of local currency bond markets, including for credit guarantees and enhancements, regional settlements and clearance, and harmonizing regional credit ratings. Existing multiple, overlapping FTAs will be consolidated into a single East Asian FTA and a regional agreement on investment will be achieved so that an East Asian Investment Area will be created.[19]

The third stage, which requires ACU to become an official currency unit, may take one of the two options — or an appropriate combination of the two. One is the "parallel-currency approach" advocated by Eichengreen (2006), which allows the ACU to freely circulate as legal tender alongside component national currencies.[20] With the increasing use of the ACU by the market as a unit of account, store of value, and medium of exchange in East Asia, the role of national currencies may diminish, and there will be greater willingness to shift the role of national currencies over to the ACU, with conditions for monetary unification naturally created. This option emphasizes the role of market forces, rather than political commitment, in dictating transition to a monetary union, which is the goal of monetary cooperation. But assigning a parallel currency role to the ACU requires a substantial political commitment.

Another option is the launch of systematic exchange rate and monetary policy coordination to create a regional monetary anchor along the line of European monetary integration. East Asian economies may develop a common framework for intraregional exchange-rate stabilization, such as an "Asian snake" or an "Asian ERM". All currencies will fluctuate freely vis-à-vis external currencies, such as the US dollar and the euro, but remain stable intraregionally through joint stabilization of individual currencies to the ACU. The mechanism should include well-defined monetary policy and intervention rules so as to provide a

---

[19] An East Asian FTA may be formed by ASEAN+3 countries or ASEAN+6 countries (including India, Australia, and New Zealand). See Kawai and Wignaraja (2008).

[20] According to Eichengreen (2006), Europe should have developed the "parallel-currency approach" but did not; it instead adopted the ERM. Eichengreen (2007c) points out the main downside of the "parallel-currency approach" being the risk of financial instability due to currency mismatches and balance sheet fragility. In Chapter 2 of this volume, Eichengreen also argues that harmonized inflation targeting as an alternative to the parallel-currency approach can go some way toward meeting the desire for stable exchange rates.

credible monetary anchor within East Asia as well as a fully elaborated very short-term liquidity facility — a counterpart of the VSTFF under the ERM of the EMS — which is large and speedy enough for frequent interventions in the region's currency markets.[21] Fiscal policy rules may also be designed to lend credibility to the exchange-rate stabilization scheme.

Whichever approach is taken, the third stage requires both significant policy initiatives and market acceptance of the ACU. In this sense, the two approaches are complementary. This transitional stage needs to be supported by much stronger institutions — including a full-fledged reserve-pooling fund (AMCF) to not only issue and manage official ACUs but also assist intraregional stability of exchange rates through facilitating a VSTFF and settle balances of interventions across central banks on a daily basis. Other institutions include a regional regulatory authority for capital markets, and a regional customs union.[22]

Overcoming the Impediments to ACU Creation

A key obstacle to the creation of an ACU index is the lack of consensus on currency weights — particularly among the "plus-three" countries of China, Japan, and Korea. This section explains the nature of these disagreements.

---

[21] Moon and Rhee (2007) argue that an ACU-based exchange-rate stabilization system should be accompanied by an emergency liquidity provision arrangement that lends without limit to cope with speculative attacks. Under the ERM of the EMS, the deutschemark emerged as the *de facto* anchor currency despite the system having been designed as a symmetric exchange-rate stabilization scheme. In Asia, it is entirely possible for the yen, the yuan, or another currency to play such an asymmetric, monetary-anchor role, but the choice will have to be left to the natural evolution of non-inflationary policymaking and credibility of the region's central banks.

[22] See Chai and Yoon (2007). A practical policy in the third stage would be to adopt a multi-track, multispeed process where economies ready for deeper policy coordination start the process, while others begin readying themselves to join. A group of economies largely fulfilling OCA conditions in East Asia — like Japan and Korea; China, Hong Kong, and Macau SAR; and Singapore, Malaysia, and Brunei Darussalam — and with sufficient political commitment, may wish to initiate subregional currency stabilization schemes. This group would intensify monetary and exchange-rate policy coordination while expecting others to join later.

Economic and Non-economic Importance of Currency Weights

If a particular currency's weight is large in the ACU basket, its movement vis-à-vis outside currencies (such as the US dollar and the euro) can significantly influence the ACU exchange rate movement against external currencies. In other words, appreciation or depreciation of a large country's currency tends to induce similar movement in the ACU exchange rate. This implies that, for the same percentage change in the exchange rate, the divergence of a particular currency's exchange-rate from the ACU is relatively small if the country is large while it is relatively large if the country is small. Hence, under an ACU-based exchange-rate stabilization system in the style of ERM, exchange rate adjustment required to reduce divergence from ACU is less for large countries than for small countries. So, there is an incentive for every economy to act like a large country by having a large weight in the currency basket.

For an ACU-based exchange-rate system to function effectively, economic stability of large countries — which are supposed to have large currency weights — is critical. If the macroeconomic performance and policies of large countries are unstable, then the ACU exchange rate may become the source of a disturbance for smaller countries as they have to import economic instability of large countries.[23] As no country wants to be disturbed by unstable economic conditions of other countries through an exchange-rate commitment, the authority of every country would wish to have a large currency weight in the ACU. Essentially, a country with the largest currency weight can exercise the leadership role under the ACU-based exchange-rate regime while a country with a small currency weight acts like a follower. Hence, every country would wish to have a large currency weight in the basket to avoid disturbances coming from the ACU-based regime.

The most important non-economic reason for wanting to have a large weight is a country's national pride, which would call for a high weight relative to peers. Every country wishes to have a weight larger than, or at least as large as, those of its peers, which could result in the total sum of more than 100%. This is impossible because the total sum cannot exceed 100% and must equal 100%.

---

[23] This suggests that the ACU-based exchange-rate regime is recommended only after sufficient credibility is secured with respect to the two large economies, Japan and China.

Role of CMI Multilateralization

The CMI multilateralization process can provide opportunities for agreeing on a key aspect of currency weights. The ASEAN+3 finance ministers agreed in May 2008 that the total size of a multilateral CMI should be at least US$80 billion and that 80% of this total should come from the "plus-three" countries and the remaining 20% from the 10 ASEAN countries. This means that the "plus-three" countries and ASEAN countries will have to decide on "shares" of individual countries' contributions to the multilateral CMI facility within the respective groups. Once they agree on these contribution "shares" in a multilateral CMI, they can become an important element that will determine the currency weights in the ACU basket. Given that the Europeans used member states' quotas in the short-term support facility of the EMS as one of the three factors — the other two being shares of GDP and intraregional trade — determining currency weights in the ECU, a similar idea can be applied to the creation of an ACU.

Table 5.6 shows that, under the bilateral swap arrangements (BSA) of the current CMI, total contributions are $84 billion, and the contributions made by the "plus-three" countries and ASEAN countries are, respectively, $73 billion (87% of the total) and $11 billion (13%). If the ASEAN Swap Arrangement (ASA) of $2 billion is added to the BSAs, the "plus-three" countries contribute 85% of the overall total ($86 billion) and ASEAN countries 15%. The contribution shares for Japan, China, and Korea are respectively 44%, 19%, and 22% of the overall total.

Once a new set of contribution shares in a multilateral CMI is agreed upon, several approaches are possible to come up with currency weights in an ACU. The first, simple approach could be to use these shares as initial currency weights and adjust them gradually over time so that they will eventually reflect the economic and financial realities of the individual countries in the region. The second approach is to adopt currency weights as suggested in this chapter, which might be acceptable to ASEAN+3 members as long as these calculated weights are not so different from the contribution shares in a new multilateral CMI. The third approach is to regard the CMI contribution shares as the fourth factor determining the ACU currency weights — together with shares of GDP, trade, and financial activity. The key point here is that the creation of a new, multilateral CMI is likely to ease the key impediment to ACU creation.

Table 5.6. Current status of BSAs under CMI (as of January 2008), US$ billion.

To: From:	China	Japan	Korea	Indonesia	Malaysia	Philippines	Singapore	Thailand	Total
China	—	3.0[a]	4.0[a]	4.0	1.5	2.0[a]		2.0	16.5
Japan	3.0[a]	—	13.0[a]	6.0	1.0[b]	6.0	3.0	6.0	38.0
Korea	4.0[a]	8.0[a]	—	2.0	1.5	2.0		1.0	18.5
Indonesia			2.0	—					2.0
Malaysia			1.5		—				1.5
Philippines		0.5	2.0			—			2.5
Singapore		1.0					—		1.0
Thailand		3.0	1.0					—	4.0
BSA Total	7.0	15.5	23.5	12.0	4.0	10.0	3.0	9.0	84.0
ASA									2.0

Source: Data from the Japanese Ministry of Finance website.

Notes: [a] The agreements are in local currencies, and the amounts are US dollar equivalents and [b] There is also a US$2.5 billion commitment (made on August 18, 1999) under the New Miyazawa Initiative.

Benefits of an ACU for Japan and China

There are benefits in creating an ACU or its index for the key countries in the group, Japan and China. For Japan, the yen's role can be preserved within an ACU basket. This is an important consideration given that yen internationalization has not proceeded in a significant way over the last 15 years and the relative role of the yen may decline over time because of the trend rise of China and other emerging market economies.

For China, the concern, or even fear, held in neighboring countries — particularly in ASEAN — that the financial influence of China and, hence, the yuan will continue to rise without bound can be contained by joining the ACU basket. As the size of Chinese GDP (based on nominal exchange rates) is expected to overtake that of Japan, it is natural to expect that the yuan will become the dominant currency in East Asia. But it would be more comforting to the rest of East Asia, particularly for ASEAN countries, if the yuan participates in a multilateral currency basket, such as the ACU, and plays its fair role in this basket. Perhaps, it is not China's intention to give the impression to the rest of East Asia and the world that it will try to promote the yuan as the sole key currency in East Asia. No action on the part of the Chinese authorities at this point may send the wrong message that China wishes to see the yuan dominate East Asian monetary affairs.

Views of the United States

It is well known that the United States was against the Japanese proposition made in 1997 to create an AMF on grounds of moral hazard and duplication. The United States argued that an East Asian economy hit by a currency crisis would bypass the tough conditionality of the IMF and receive easy money from the AMF, thereby creating potential for moral hazard, and that an AMF would be redundant in the presence of an effective global crisis manager, the IMF. If the United States holds a negative view on the role of an ACU, this may constitute another impediment to the birth of an ACU.

The US position was unclear when the possibility of creating an ACU was discussed in 2006. It was mentioned that the United States would not welcome the emergence of an ACU as it may undermine the key currency role of the US dollar in East Asia. However, the US view was eventually clarified by Adams (2006), Under Secretary for International Affairs of the US Treasury at that time. He stated: "With respect to an Asian Currency Unit (ACU), there has been some confusion about the US position on this topic. We do not see the ACU as a competitor to the dollar. We believe that greater exchange-rate flexibility is desirable for the region, but are open-minded as to whether that involves currency cooperation within the region." On broader regional financial cooperation, while he wants to see more "clarity on the CMI" with regard to the amounts available without IMF programs and the conditions imposed by CMI creditors, he stated "we support regional cooperation that is consistent with multilateral frameworks."

The Way Forward

To support the ongoing process of market-driven economic and financial integration among East Asian economies, more systematic, coordinated institution building is clearly needed. While several ACU indexes can be constructed for different groups of Asian economies, ASEAN+3 is a natural starting point because of its ongoing financial cooperation efforts. Once introduced and made operative, the ACU can become an important tool in regional economic surveillance, help deepen Asian financial markets — particularly for local currency-denominated bonds — and contribute to further monetary and financial cooperation. It is clearly important for the region's finance ministers and central bank governors to strengthen coordination on these initiatives.

One of the most serious impediments to ACU creation — lack of consensus on currency weights in an ACU basket — can be resolved once policymakers make progress on CMI multilateralization. The reason is that in this process they need to decide on contribution "shares" in a multilateral CMI. These agreed shares may be simply used as the initial currency weights or be regarded as an important factor — together with shares of GDP, trade, and financial activity — determining currency weights. The fact that ASEAN+3 members — particularly China, Japan, and Korea — decide on shares among themselves will remove their fear that an international organization, like the Asian Development Bank (ADB), may unilaterally decide currency weights. It will make the discussion of creating an ACU much easier and smoother.

The creation of an ACU by itself, however, does not automatically guarantee the emergence of ACU-denominated bonds or the beginning of close exchange-rate policy coordination. East Asia has yet to achieve a significant economic and structural convergence, create resilient and open financial markets, and build adequate regional institutions to support policy coordination. Policymakers have yet to be convinced of the net gains of enhanced exchange-rate policy coordination — stable intraregional exchange rates — despite the perceived costs due to a potential loss of sovereignty over national monetary policymaking.

The impetus toward regional exchange-rate policy coordination may come sooner rather than later if the US dollar depreciates sharply against East Asian (and other major) currencies. This can happen in the unwinding process of global payments imbalances, in the financial turmoil emanating from the US subprime crisis, and/or in the face of surges in private capital flows into the region — under the expectation of a rapid slowdown of US economic growth and relatively healthy East Asian economic growth. If East Asian economies must accept currency appreciation against the dollar, they had better do so collectively while maintaining intraregional rate stability, so that the costs of economic adjustment can be spread among them and, hence, reduced for each of them. This type of informal policy coordination — which requires Chinese yuan's greater exchange-rate flexibility — has the potential to create an East Asian monetary zone, parallel to that observed in Europe after the collapse of the Bretton Woods System in the early 1970s. In this context, an ACU can play a significant role in boosting policy coordination across East Asia.

CHAPTER 6
Asian Monetary Unification: Lessons from Europe[1]

Paul De Grauwe

Introduction

The financial crisis of 1997–98 was a fundamental challenge to Asia's policy status quo. Stable, competitively valued exchange rates had been a pillar of the region's highly successful model of export-led growth, but many Asian countries now found that in a world of free capital mobility they were no longer able to keep their currencies stable. Resist as they might, speculative attacks forced them to devalue or let their exchange rates float. In the short run this led to significant macroeconomic dislocations and disrupted trade flows. Neither consequence was happy for a set of Asian governments whose legitimacy rested on their ability to deliver rapid economic growth nor for a set of economies whose manufacturing industry depended on exports as a principal source of demand.

A series of initiatives was therefore undertaken to prevent a recurrence of such events. The most important of these was the Chiang Mai Initiative (CMI), announced by the Finance Ministers of ASEAN, China, Japan, and South Korea in May 2000. The CMI extended the network of bilateral short-term credit arrangements that had existed among a subset of ASEAN countries to this larger ASEAN+3 grouping. It also lent impetus to the development of an economic review and policy dialog process aimed at proactively eliminating macroeconomic and financial disequilibria that may lead to the recurrence of crises.[2]

At the same time, there is a widespread view that these initiatives are not enough to successfully shield Asian countries from monetary disturbances.

---

[1] I am grateful to Barry Eichengreen, Hae-Sik Park, Kyung-Soo Kim, and Yeongseop Rhee for their useful comments and suggestions.
[2] See Xu (2004) and the chapter by Chai and Moon in this volume.

Also needed, in this view, is a mechanism for permanently locking the exchange rates between their currencies. And the only way of credibly achieving that goal, it is argued, is by creating an Asian monetary union.[3]

In this chapter, I ask whether Europe's experience with monetary integration contains lessons relevant to this Asian debate. I start by comparing economic conditions in East Asia with those in the Euro area with an eye toward determining whether Asia is less well suited for monetary unification. The finding of this analysis, somewhat surprisingly, is that East Asia comes at least as close as Europe to satisfying the standard preconditions for monetary unification. The main differences between Europe and Asia are not in economic and financial structure but, rather, in the institutional sphere. Thus, the important lessons from European experience concern how an institutional framework supportive of the transition to monetary union can be put in place.

East Asia is as Much an Optimum Currency Area as Europe

The conditions needed to guarantee the sustainability of a monetary union are familiar from the literature on optimum currency areas.[4] They can be summarized in terms of three concepts: symmetry, flexibility, and integration. To start with, countries in a monetary union should experience macroeconomic shocks that are reasonably symmetric (or similar) to those experienced in the rest of the monetary zone, since they are now consigned to an identical monetary response. In addition, they should have sufficient labor market flexibility to accommodate asymmetric shocks, given the absence of an independent country-specific monetary instrument. Finally, the participating countries should have a sufficient degree of trade integration to ensure that the convenience and efficiency advantages of a common currency (whose most obvious benefit is to facilitate trade) dominate the costs.

Figure 6.1 measures the degree of economic integration in East Asia and the Euro area, comparing the exports of East Asian countries to the rest of East Asia as a percent of their GDP with the exports of European Union (EU) countries with the rest of the EU also as a percent of GDP. The overall finding is that most East Asian countries are

---

[3] Genberg (2006) describes a strategy that could be used to move toward monetary union in East Asia. See also Sanchez (2005).

[4] Mundell (1961), McKinnon (1963), and Kenen (1969).

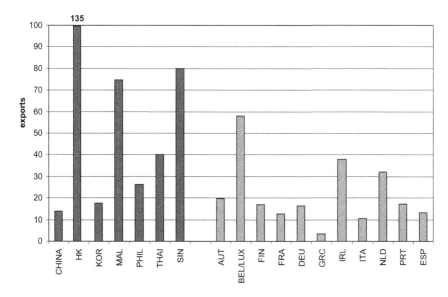

Figure 6.1. Intra-regional exports of goods and services, East Asia and EU as percent of GDP (2003).
Source: IMF, IFS, and Xu (2004).
Note: The exports of the East Asian countries are to ASEAN plus China, Korea, and Japan. Data for China relate to 2001.

relatively well integrated in terms of trade with their Asian neighbors, when the integration of European countries with their European neighbors is taken as the metric. Indeed, some countries in East Asia have exceptionally high integration ratios; Hong Kong, for example, has a ratio exceeding 100 percent. This very high ratio reflects the fact that exports derive from production data (which include imports), while GDP is computed on the basis of value added (which excludes imports). Hong Kong's exports are, to a large extent, transit trade with little value added. As a result, its export/GDP ratio exceeds 100 percent. But that a substantial share of Hong Kong's trade is made up of re-exports of goods imported from China does not change the point. Currency stability is unusually valuable for an economy that specializes in transit trade. Thus, a country in Hong Kong's position is likely to benefit substantially from a common regional currency, other things being equal.

A variety of analytical and econometric methods have been used to identify symmetric and asymmetric shocks. The consensus emerging from that literature is that Asian countries do not experience more asymmetry than the members of the Euro area.[5] For example, Xu (2004) computes the percentage of the variation in demand and supply shocks that can be attributed to common shocks. These percentages are computed by first extracting the shocks using the Blanchard-Quah structural VAR procedure. The supply and demand shocks thereby obtained are then subjected to a factor analysis, which allows estimation of the common component in movements of these shocks.[6] The share of the total variation captured by this common component can be interpreted as expressing the degree of symmetry in the shocks. Xu's results are summarized in Figs. 6.2 and 6.3,

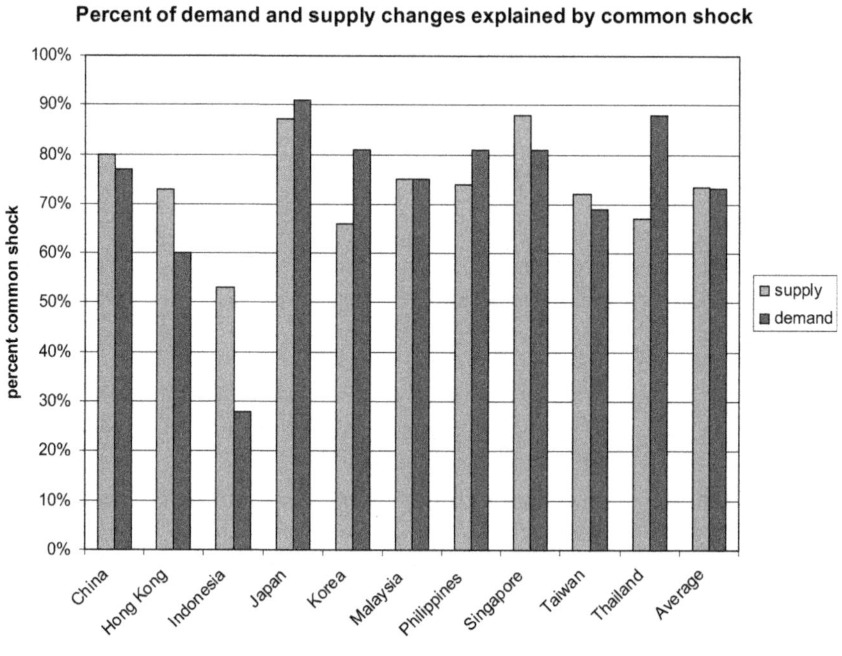

Percent of demand and supply changes explained by common shock

Figure 6.2. Symmetry of shocks in East Asia.
Source: Xu (2004).

---

[5] See Eichengreen and Bayoumi (1999), Cheung and Yuen (2003), Xu (2004), Shin and Sohn (2006), and Sato and Zhang (2006).

[6] This approach is widely used, but is subject to an important criticism. This is that the shocks identified as demand shocks are in fact temporary shocks, while the shocks identified as supply shocks are in fact permanent shocks.

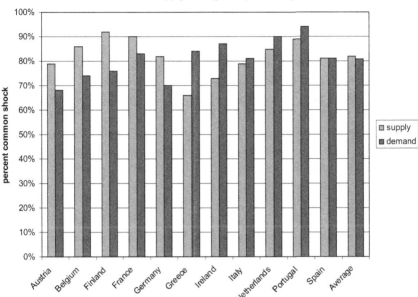

Figure 6.3. Symmetry of shocks in the Eurozone.
Source: Xu (2004).

where Fig. 6.2 shows the relevant percentages for the East Asian countries and Fig. 6.3 shows them for the Euro area. Strikingly, the degree of symmetry of shocks of the Asian countries appears to be only slightly lower than that of the Euro area countries.[7]

Thus, by at least two of the standard optimum currency area (OCA) criteria — symmetry and integration — East Asia seems to be close to an optimum currency area, assuming that the Eurozone is a good benchmark. In addition, since it appears that the flexibility of East Asian labor markets is at least as high if not higher than Europe's, it would appear that East Asia comes at least as close as Europe to forming an optimum currency area, at least when the question is answered on the standard economic and financial grounds.

---

[7] The outlier is Indonesia whose demand and supply shocks do not seem to be well synchronized with the rest of Asia.

Then Why Do We Not Observe Monetary Union in Asia?

If the economic conditions for monetary unification are in place, why then has it not come about? The answer is almost surely institutional, political, and historical. In contrast to the situation in Europe, there is nearly a total absence of supranational institutions in East Asia to which nations have delegated power. And the explanation for that institutional vacuum lies in the region's distinctive history and politics.

In Europe, there already existed a long-standing integrationist tradition.[8] As a result, the destruction resulting from the Second World War fed an existing impulse for political integration which found reflection in the development of supranational institutions like the European Commission, the European Court of Justice, and the European Parliament. The creation of each of these institutions entailed some transfer of national sovereignty to the level of the union. It was the development of these supranational structures that ultimately made it possible to create yet another supranational institution with monetary powers, the European Central Bank (ECB). Not only did this inheritance make it possible to establish the ECB, but it also applied pressure and lent momentum to efforts in that direction. It follows that in order to move to a monetary union, East Asia will have to develop analogous institutions. That, in turn, will require solving some very fundamental political problems.

Only recently have economists begun to consider the institutional challenges that arise when moving to a new economic or monetary regime.[9] Proponents of the conventional wisdom had long argued that the main prerequisites for a successful monetary union were the three OCA conditions considered above plus an independent central bank. In practice, however, things were not so simple. It turned out also to be necessary to reform and create other institutions in which a country's economic and monetary arrangements can be embedded.

Moreover, institutional reform and development take time. The ECB was not just parachuted into an institutional desert. It was the culmination

---

[8] See inter alia Eichengreen (2007b), Chapter 2.

[9] This new awareness was importantly stimulated by the transition of previously communist countries into market economies. There is a large literature by now stressing the importance of designing the right institutions. See Aslund (2007) for a fascinating account of the Russian transition.

of a long process of institution building. A bit of European history serves to illustrate the point.

A Brief History of European Monetary Integration

Monetary cooperation in Europe started in 1950 with the creation of the European Payments Union (EPU). This was an arrangement among the 18 members of the Organization for European Economic Cooperation (OEEC), the precursor of the present-day OECD. It responded to the post-war dollar shortage and the absence of currency convertibility that hindered efforts to rebuild the earlier system of multilateral settlements. In the absence of convertibility and hard-currency reserves, each European country was forced into the position of balancing its trade with each of its European partners. This inability to rebuild the prewar system of multi-lateral settlements constituted an important obstacle to the postwar reconstruction and recovery of the European economy.

The EPU solved this problem by setting up a multilateral clearing system in which credits accumulated in the course of trade with one country could be used to cancel debts incurred in trade with another. It also entailed a system of financial supports for countries running modest deficits with the union as a whole. For obvious reasons, this system of multilateral clearing and credits greatly facilitated the reconstruction of the prewar system of trade and payments. But, in addition, the EPU was useful as a first concrete instance of monetary cooperation. Officials from different European countries worked together on the EPU managing board to decide on the disbursal of credits and recommend adjustment measures to the countries receiving them. In effect, the EPU served as a training ground for subsequent moves to monetary integration.[10]

At the end of 1958, with the restoration of current account convertibility, the Bretton Woods System came into full operation. But Europe's monetary relations still centered on the dollar. Intraregional exchange rates were stabilized by pegging each European currency to the dollar.[11] This arrangement worked reasonably well so long as the dollar remained stable. But it collapsed in the early 1970s as US inflation accelerated, the

---

[10] The EPU became superfluous when the participating countries made their currencies convertible in 1959.

[11] Not unlike the situation in East Asia in the 1990s.

US government could not maintain a fixed dollar price of gold, and President Nixon shut the gold window, eliminating the convertibility of the dollar into gold at a fixed price for official foreign holders.

Europe's response was a series of efforts to make its own arrangements for stabilizing intraregional exchange rates. The first such attempt, the Werner Plan, was formulated in 1970 in anticipation of the subsequent collapse of the Bretton Woods System. It was an agreement among the members of the European Community, the precursor of today's EU, to peg their exchange rates bilaterally. This agreement was formally presented as a first step toward full monetary union, a goal which the signatories of the Werner Plan saw as achievable by 1980. It started with the Snake (essentially a regional variant on Bretton Woods), which gave way to the evocatively named Snake in the Tunnel and then the Snake in the Lake. This series of expedients notwithstanding, the plan collapsed in the late 1970s as exchange-rate volatility and economic volatility rose to high levels owing to oil shocks, commodity price inflation, and unstable economic policies.

The second attempt at fixing exchange rates was in 1979 with the establishment of the European Monetary System (EMS). A central feature of the EMS was its Exchange Rate Mechanism (the ERM) designed to keep bilateral exchange rates within ±2.25 percent of their central parities. This mechanism operated successfully in the 1980s, though with many realignments of parities, it being possible to organize orderly realignments because of the protection from speculative attacks afforded by capital controls. But the system came under stress once capital controls were eliminated in the late 1980s and early 1990s as a result of the Single European Act designed to create an integrated internal market not just in merchandise but also labor and, importantly, capital. The result was the crisis of 1992–93, when a series of member states were forced to devalue involuntarily and some were forced into the drastic step of abandoning their participation in the system, either temporarily (as in the case of Italy) or permanently (as in the case of the United Kingdom). The community's response was to widen fluctuation bands from ±2.25 percent to ±15 percent, transforming the system into one tantamount to floating. With a strong currency moving as much as 15 percent above its central parity but a weak one moving down by that same amount, bilateral rates might fluctuate by as much as 30 percent. (For more institutional details, see Appendix 6.1.)

This inability to maintain pegged but adjustable exchange rates in this brave new world of high capital mobility effectively forced European countries to move either to more flexible exchange rates or irrevocably fixed pegs. Their choice, in other words, was to resign themselves to a world in which currencies would fluctuate by as much as ±15 percent, or to undertake a forced march to monetary union. Exchange rates as variable as this, in the majority view, were incompatible with the larger project of establishing a single European market. Starting in 1993, a growing number of European countries therefore began giving serious consideration to abandoning monetary sovereignty in order to achieve exchange-rate stability through the creation of a monetary union. The remainder of the decade was dominated by the transition to this union, which was successfully launched on 1 January 1999.

From this brief review two conclusions follow. First, the immediate objective of monetary cooperation in the EU was the maintenance of exchange-rate stability. This makes it important to directly address the question of why exchange-rate stability figured so prominently in the early stages of monetary integration. Second, pegging the exchange rate was seen as a preliminary step toward full monetary union. Although it can be said that all these attempts at pegging the exchange rates failed, it is also true that they were ultimately successful in establishing a glide path to monetary union. They did so by fostering the further development of existing supranational institutions and by encouraging the creation of new ones. The special value of these exchange-rate arrangements was as institution-building devices.

Exchange-Rate Pegging as Institution Building

A basic question for any multilateral fixed exchange-rate system is how to set the systemwide money stock and interest rate. This is the so-called $n - 1$ problem — that in a system of n countries there are only $n - 1$ independent exchange rates.[12] Consequently, $n - 1$ monetary authorities will be forced to adjust their monetary policy instruments to maintain a fixed exchange rate, while one monetary authority will be free to set its monetary policy independently. In effect, the system has a single degree of freedom.

---

[12] There are more exchange rates (actually the number is $n(n - 1)/2$). Arbitrage, however, ensures that only $n - 1$ are independent.

The question is how this degree of freedom will be utilized. Will it be given to a particular central bank which is then free to set its monetary policies independently? This was the solution under the Bretton Woods System, in which the United States assumed the role of the nth country. Or will this degree of freedom be shared by the countries participating in the exchange-rate arrangement, requiring cooperation in deciding the common level of interest rates?

The architects of the EMS had envisaged a cooperative system, but things did not work out this way. Very quickly the German Bundesbank acquired the single degree of freedom; it set the level of interest rates systemwide, and other central banks followed. The EMS evolved into an asymmetric arrangement very much like the Bretton Woods System.

Thus, although the attempt to design a cooperative system failed, the initiative was successful as an institution-building device. By putting the Bundesbank at the center of the system, it was easier at a later stage to create a ECB, which would be a close copy (some would say a carbon copy) of the German central bank. This approach was encouraged by the positive record of the Bundesbank in maintaining price stability, this being a priority of the designers of the ECB in the 1990s. The formula embedded in the statute of the Bundesbank was political independence and the primacy of price stability as an objective of monetary policies. Given the central position of the Bundesbank in the EMS, it was easy to translate these institutional features into the design of the ECB.

The EMS was also an institution-building device in another sense. Despite the dominance of Germany in the system, there was the need for regular consultation among the central banks participating in the ERM. Mechanisms were therefore developed to systematize that cooperation; these included the Committee of Central Bank Governors and the Monetary Committee. These institutions cultivated a culture of cooperation and mutual understanding that would prove to be very valuable later.[13]

Other pre-existing institutions, in particular the Economic and Financial Affairs Council of the European Union (ECOFIN), obtained greater stature as a result of their role in the operation of the EMS. As part of the executive branch of the EU, ECOFIN finance ministers could make decisions by a qualified majority. The ECOFIN was instrumental in

---

[13] See Gros and Thygesen (1999) for a detailed analysis of the development and functioning of these institutions.

organizing orderly realignments within ERM and in doing so helped to foster a culture of cooperation. In this way cooperation in exchange-rate management in the context of the EMS led to intensified use of existing European institutions and encouraged the creation of new ones. All this laid the foundation for an institutional infrastructure without which the subsequent monetary union would not have been possible.

In Europe, monetary cooperation focused initially on the maintenance of exchange-rate stability. Why was this objective so salient? In part, the answer is the high degree of economic integration already achieved in other areas. Such an integration was extensive by the 1960s and 1970s, raising the danger of trade disruptions when exchange rates changed. Also important was the Common Agricultural Policy (CAP), under which a unified system of price supports was used to maintain orderly conditions in the community's single market in agricultural goods. The Council of Ministers of Agriculture set prices for the main agricultural products, expressed in the European Unit of Account (EUA), which later became the ECU. National prices were then obtained by converting the EUA into national currency. But when the bilateral exchange rates within the EU became volatile in the 1970s, these arrangements became problematic. Countries that saw their currency depreciate (like in France and Italy) experienced strong and immediate increases in the prices of agricultural products, while countries with appreciating currencies (as in Germany) saw prices decline. These movements were strongly resisted by farmers, consumers, and officials in the respective countries.

A corrective mechanism (a system of "green exchange rates") was instituted to eliminate the impact of exchange-rate changes on agricultural prices. This mechanism, however, required the use of tariffs and subsidies on imports of agricultural products. It also threatened to roll back the market integration already achieved in the agricultural sector. As a result, the pressure to go back to fixed exchange rates remained an underlying drive of monetary cooperation.

Lessons for East Asia

Compared to Europe, East Asia lacks the supranational institutions necessary to provide a political basis for monetary unification, although it adequately meets the standard economic and financial criteria. However, recent research suggests that, if anything, the current position underestimates the conformance of economic and financial conditions with the imperatives of monetary unification. It further predicts that economic and financial conditions will adapt when independent national monetary policies are foregone. The optimum currency area conditions are endogenous, in other words.[14]

One might make an analogous argument about the institutional preconditions. The decision to set up institutions for monetary cooperation may create a political dynamic in which further institutional integration will occur. Although the political preconditions for monetary unification are not in place in East Asia today, steps toward deeper monetary cooperation may help to install them. This strategy was effective in Europe, as described above. Seeing if it can work in East Asia requires that political leaders take the first steps.

If the history of European monetary unification is a good guide, the right place for such steps is exchange-rate management. Until recently, pegging to the US dollar has been the vehicle for maintaining exchange-rate stability in East Asia. The next step, then, would be to set up an exchange-rate arrangement similar to the ERM. This would set in motion the process of institution building necessary for further steps toward monetary union.

As Europe's experience makes clear, it is essential that Asia pursue other dimensions of the integration process and build institutions analogous to ECOFIN. The CMI and Asian Bond Market Initiative hold promise in this regard, although neither focuses on exchange-rate management per se — the CMI being concerned with financial stability and the Asian Bond Market Initiative focusing on the development of debt markets. This suggests that perhaps Asia should not simply follow Europe's example, where cooperation on exchange rates formed the basis for institution building, but rather focus on the financial stability and development issues that are equally salient for the region.

Conclusion

Following World War II, few observers predicted that Europe would embark on the road to political and monetary unification. The legacy of war seemed to preclude reconciliation. Yet reconciliation happened, partly

---

[14] See Frankel and Rose (1998) and De Grauwe and Mongelli (2005).

because of the efforts in the 1950s of a small elite to start down that road. There is no clearer example of path dependence.

If there is a lesson for East Asia from Europe, it is that the longest journey starts with the first step. A first step in the direction of monetary and financial cooperation can help to cultivate the attitudes and develop the institutions necessary to support subsequent steps. At the end of this particular journey is monetary unification. This end will not be reached in Asia overnight, but it is achievable.

Appendix 6.1. The European Monetary System: Some Institutional Features

The EMS was instituted in 1979. It was a response to the large exchange-rate variability of community currencies during the 1970s, which was seen as endangering the integration process in Europe.[15] The EMS consisted of two elements: the ERM and the ECU.

Like the Bretton Woods System, the ERM was an adjustable peg system. That is, countries participating in the ERM determined an official exchange rate (central rate) for their currencies, and a band around these central rates within which the exchange rates could fluctuate freely. This band was set at 2.25 percent and −2.25 percent around the central rate for most member countries (Belgium, Denmark, France, Germany, Ireland, and the Netherlands). Italy was allowed to use a larger band of fluctuation (6 percent and −6 percent) until 1990 when it moved to the narrower band. The three newcomers to the system, Spain (1989), the United Kingdom (1990), and Portugal (1992), also used the wider band. The United Kingdom dropped out of the system in September 1992. In August 1993, the band of fluctuation was raised to 15 percent and −15 percent. On 1 January 1999, the EMS ceased to exist.

When the limits of the band (the margins) were reached, the central banks of the currencies involved were committed to intervene so as to maintain the exchange rate within the band. This intervention was called "marginal" intervention (i.e., intervention at the margins of the band). The commitment to intervene at the margins, however, was not absolute.

---

[15] For an account of the discussions that led to the establishment of the EMS, see Ludlow (1982). For a more detailed description of some institutional features of the system, see van Ypersele (1985).

Countries could, after consultation with the other members of the system, decide to change the parity rates of their currency (to realign). Realignments were frequent during the first half of the 1980s, when more than 10 took place. They became much less frequent after the middle of the 1980s. During the years 1987–92, no realignment took place. In 1992–93, major crises erupted, which led to several realignments. In August 1993, the nature of the ERM was changed drastically by the increase of the band of fluctuations to 15 percent and −15 percent.

The second feature of the EMS was the existence of the ECU. The ECU was defined as a basket of currencies of the countries that are members of the EMS. (This was a larger group of countries than the ERM members. It included all the EU countries except Austria, Finland, and Sweden.)

The value of the ECU in terms of currency i (the ECU rate of currency i) was defined as follows:

$$ECU_i = \sum_j a_j S_{ji} \qquad (1)$$

where a_j is the amount of currency j in the basket; S_{ji} is the price of currency j in units of currency i (the bilateral exchange rate).

Since the a_{js} were fixed, this definition of the ECU implies that an appreciating currency will see its percentage share in the ECU increase, while a depreciating currency will see its percentage share decline. This feature was deemed unacceptable for political reasons. As a result, every five years the amounts (the a_{js}) in the basket were adjusted, i.e., they were increased for the depreciating currencies and reduced for the appreciating currencies. This feature may have solved a political problem, but it created another problem: the poor attractiveness of the ECU as a currency to be used in market transactions.

On 1 January 1999, the ECU was transformed into the euro at the rate of 1 ECU = 1 euro. When the euro became a currency in its own right, the basket definition ceased to exist.

CHAPTER 7

Managing Foreign Exchange Reserves: The Case of China

Yu Yongding

Introduction

East Asian countries have accumulated massive foreign exchange since their 1997–98 financial crisis. Reserve accumulation has provided insurance against financial risks, but it also has created dilemmas for central banks. It has sounded alarm bells in the developed world, where the creation of sovereign wealth funds (SWFs) by developing countries has become a *cause célèbre*.

This chapter explores these issues in the case of China. It argues that far from being shrewd in advancing a hidden strategic agenda, Chinese officials, in fact, are confused by the rapid accumulation of reserves and face serious challenges in their efforts to manage them.

I start by describing China's growth strategy and explaining how it has led to the accumulation of reserves. I then identify the problems created by the country's chronic current- and capital-account surpluses. Next, I turn to the management of reserves and the issues raised by the creation of a SWF. In conclusion, I consider the implications for the development of capital markets and regional financial cooperation in Asia.

Growth and Reserve Accumulation

Two rationales for reserve accumulation dominate the scholarly and policy literatures. The first, given expression by Feldstein (1998), sees reserve accumulation as part of a strategy for strengthening a country's liquidity position and protecting it against financial instability. This goal can be attained by three means: limiting short-term debt, creating a collateralized credit facility (something that was ultimately achieved in Asia through the Chiang Mai Initiative (CMI)), and accumulating international reserves. The second rationale, noted by Rodrik (2006) is old-fashioned mercantilism. Rightly or wrongly, governments see large reserves as a source of power in the international system.

Even before Feldstein *et al.* elaborated these motives, China had embarked on the process of reserve accumulation. Almost certainly both the self-insurance and mercantilist motives were at work. In addition, however, there is a third explanation for the growth of China's reserves: the country's reserve accumulation, I argue in this chapter, was a concomitant of the particular growth strategy pursued from the 1980s.

The East Asian growth model has two distinguishing features. One is a high investment rate supported by a high saving rate and supplemented by capital inflows. The other is export promotion which results in trade and current-account surpluses. While the East Asian model has been strikingly successful at raising living standards, it is susceptible to reversals in capital flows, a fact dramatically illustrated by the Asian financial crisis.

The Chinese growth model resembles the East Asian growth model but for two related differences. Though China exhibits a high investment rate supported by high saving and foreign direct investment (FDI) inflows, investment is less than savings — capital flows out from the country on balance. And while Chinese growth is export driven, the rate of growth of exports is even higher than the rate of growth of imports.[1]

The most important advantage of the Chinese model, compared to its East Asian counterpart, is its resilience. It is difficult to imagine that a balance-of-payments and currency crisis could hit China. However, this resilience is achieved at a price: a relatively low efficiency of resource allocation. The most important expression of this is the existence of chronic current- and capital-account-surpluses, which are anomalous for what is still a relatively poor country.

---

[1] There are also other differences, such as the dominance of state-owned banks and the prevalence of capital controls. But these are of second-order importance for the current discussion.

What's Wrong with the Chinese Model?

There is no question but that China's growth strategy has been a striking success. But the country has paid a price in terms of environmental damage, depletion of energy and natural resources, and social tension. These problems also raise questions about the sustainability of the model going forward. What were engines of growth in the past may become brakes in the future unless China can adapt its strategy.

These observations apply specifically to the problem of reserve accumulation. A poor country in the early stages of economic development would normally be expected to run a current account deficit and capital-account surplus. That capital-account surplus allows it to finance a portion of its investment abroad while freeing up additional resources for consumption. The current account deficit allows it to import advanced capital goods and technology.

More generally, one can imagine a nation's balance of payments as passing through six stages (Crowther, 1957):

1. *Young debtor nation.* Because domestic savings are scarce, a poor country will procure goods and capital from abroad. Imports will exceed exports, and interest payments will be made by further borrowing. The result is trade and current account deficits. Because those deficits are financed by imports of capital, the economy becomes a net foreign debtor.
2. *Mature debtor nation.* In this second stage, export-oriented manufacturing begins to develop. However, the country's foreign earnings do not yet cover interest payments on the external debt. The trade and current account balances remain in deficit, while the capital account is still in surplus.
3. *Debt repayment nation.* As exports continue to grow, the trade surplus begins to exceed interest payments. The current account therefore moves into surplus. The capital account, however, remains in surplus as well.
4. *Young creditor nation.* As the surplus on current account swells and external debt is paid down, the country becomes a net foreign creditor. The balance on net interest payments becomes positive and the capital account moves into deficit, reflecting rising foreign investment.
5. *Mature creditor nation.* As foreign assets continue to grow, a rising share of net interest income is devoted to consumption. Meanwhile, with the aging of the population, savings and labor-force-participation

rates begin to decline. The trade balance moves into deficit but, given net interest earnings from abroad, the current account remains in surplus.

6. *Credit disposition nation.* In this final stage, marked by the further rise in consumption relative to production, the current account moves into deficit. The country runs down its net foreign assets to lower, sustainable levels.

How does China fit into this schema? Since the early 1990s, the country has been running a current-account surplus, a trade surplus, and an investment-income deficit. It can therefore be regarded as in the third stage of Crowther's schema (as shown in Fig. 7.1). But it has remained there

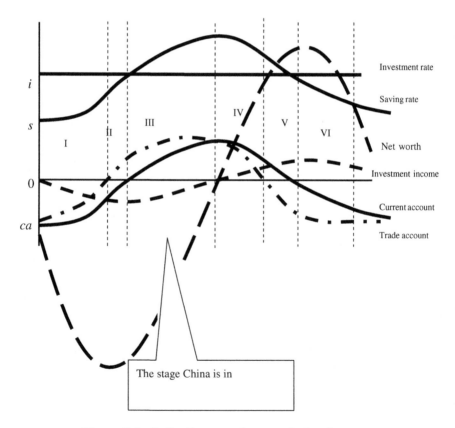

The stage China is in

Figure 7.1. Stylized stages of economic development.
Note: All variables are normalized by GDP (expressed as ratios).

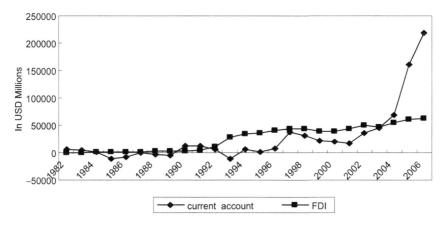

Figure 7.2. China's twin surpluses.

for an unusually long time. This is one way of understanding why the country's international economic policies are controversial. Indeed, China may be the only country in recorded history to have run both current- and capital-account surpluses for as long as 16 years (Fig. 7.2).[2]

What if anything is wrong with running current- and capital-account surpluses? First, the fact that the 100th poorest country in the world in per capita GDP terms is the third largest capital exporter is, in some sense, fundamentally perverse. One normally would expect capital to flow from rich countries, where it is relatively abundant, to poor countries, where it is relatively scarce. Second, that the third largest FDI-attracting country fails to transform capital inflows into current account deficits is further indicative of resource misallocation and of lower levels of consumption than it might enjoy otherwise. Third, the country's foreign exchange reserves are losing value as a result of the depreciation of foreign currencies against the renminbi, inflation in the United States, and American credit market problems. (For a schematic view, see Fig. 7.3.)

The fact that China is running twin current- and capital-account surpluses means that the country more than fully finances its economic development. Contrary to Crowther's schema, China has failed to utilize

---

[2] The only exception is 1993, when China had a current-account deficit due to overheating. It is worth noting that capital inflows into China also include foreign loans, portfolio investment, trade credits, leasing, and so on. Because FDI dominates capital inflows in the 1990s and onward, only FDI will be discussed here.

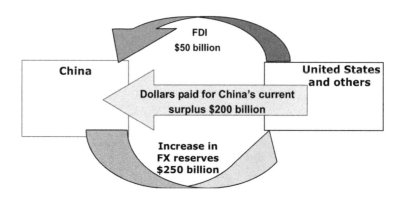

Figure 7.3. China's FDI is financed by China itself.

a penny of foreign resources despite its still relatively low per capita GDP. To the contrary, it is subsidizing spending by the United States and other high-income countries to the tune of $200 billion per annum.

Another disturbing observation is that China's net investment income account was persistently negative until 2005, this despite the fact that the country has been a net capital exporter for a decade and a half and was the sixth largest net foreign creditor in the world. (see Fig. 7.4.) Although Japan similarly has a less-than-impressive record of returns on its foreign investment, it at least has a positive net international income position when it is running a trade surplus.

Where China's trade surplus has grabbed headlines in the news media, less attention has been paid to the fact that the capital-account surplus contributed more importantly to its accumulation of foreign exchange reserves before 2005 — and that this had been true for decades. Foreign direct investment inflows jumped from $4 billion in 1991 to $11 billion in 1992 and $27 billion in 1993. Since 1996, annual FDI inflows have persisted at levels around $40–50 billion. The Chinese government expects that in the next five years annual FDI inflows will continue to run at perhaps $50 billion per annum.

Why has China attracted so much FDI despite its extraordinarily high savings rate? While economy-wide savings are high, it remains difficult for many potential importers of capital goods to raise funds domestically for purchases overseas, reflecting the underdevelopment of the country's capital markets. Instead, enterprises sell the foreign exchange obtained via investment transactions with joint-venture partners to the central bank

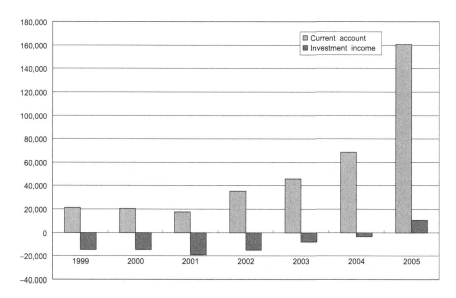

Figure 7.4. China's current-account surplus and investment-account deficit (million of US dollars).

(the People's Bank of China, or PBOC) and use the domestic currency thereby obtained to purchase capital goods produced locally. In this manner, FDI and foreign exchange reserves rise, but without offsetting changes in the current account.

Essentially, China's savings are transformed into investment using the intermediation services of foreign capital markets. To illustrate, suppose there are two provinces: Province A runs a current-account surplus, while Province B does the opposite. In a market economy with well-functioning financial markets, the foreign exchange reserves obtained by the first province can be used to finance imports from the second. If the current-account surplus of Province A is greater than the need for foreign exchange of Province B, then the country as a whole will run a current-account surplus and a capital-account deficit. If, on the other hand, the current-account surplus of Province A is smaller than the need for foreign exchange of Province B, then the country as a whole will run a current-account deficit and a capital-account surplus.

But in China's case, Province B does not obtain foreign exchange from Province A via the intermediation of domestic financial markets, due to the existence of market imperfections.[3] Instead, it relies on FDI from the United States and other foreign countries. Province A sells its surplus foreign exchange to the State Administration of Foreign Exchange (SAFE), which in turn uses the foreign exchange to purchase treasury bills and other US assets. The country's foreign exchange receipts are thereby recycled via the US capital market, financing Province B's trade deficit. Province A's trade surplus is much larger than Province B's trade deficit. Thus, the country as a whole runs both trade and capital-account surpluses.

The policy implication is that China's twin current- and capital-account surpluses can be eliminated only by deepening market reform and scrapping the market-distorting policies that artificially favor exports and FDI inflows.

Reducing the Growth of International Reserves

In 1995, China's foreign exchange reserves exceeded US$100 billion. (See Fig. 7.5.) As early as 1997, I published an article calling for the end of trade- and FDI-attracting practices aimed at accumulating international reserves (Yu, 1997). I likened the pattern to the poor lending money to the rich at low interest rates and then borrowing the money back at greater cost to themselves.

Unfortunately, the Asian financial crisis lent further encouragement to those advocating policies of reserve accumulation. In the wake of the crisis, the further increase in China's foreign exchange reserves was also an unintentional consequence of the government's efforts to fight deflation, which aimed at promoting exports as well as boosting domestic demand. Since 2003, reserve accumulation has accelerated further. This should not be seen as resulting from any new policy initiative on the part of the Chinese government; rather, it is the unintended consequence of a growth strategy adopted some 25 years earlier and still in place. By now, a trade structure dominated by processing trade has been firmly established. Foreign-funded enterprises (FFEs) producing for export markets have sprung up across China, and domestic enterprises have succeeded in integrating themselves into international production networks as assemblers and processors.

---

[3] This is also an issue of political economy.

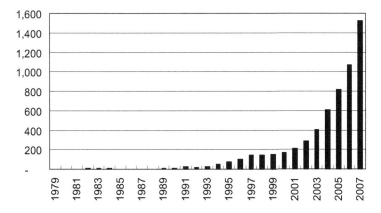

Figure 7.5. China's foreign exchange reserves (billion USD).

Instead of mercantilism or self-insurance, it is these aspects of the country's economic development that explain China's continuing accumulation of reserves. To the extent that the country remains trapped in its old growth strategy, it has no choice but to run current- and capital-account surpluses whether it likes it or not. If the government curtails its intervention in the foreign exchange market, the exchange rate will appreciate and the accumulation of reserves will be slow. But this will disrupt the processing trade and assembly operations described above, threatening economic growth. Hence, important stakeholders in the enterprise and government sectors resist calls for radical change.[4]

A more plausible scenario is gradual adjustment and reform. The starting point would be the elimination of policies aimed at promoting exports and attracting FDI. The government could overhaul tax policies encouraging energy use, resource extraction, and environment pollution, which have led to the mispricing of resources and subsidized exports. Social and income policies should be introduced to limit inequality and

---

[4] This is evident in policy toward the exchange rate. In early 2003, the issue of appreciation was raised and rejected because of the "fear of appreciation". In 2004, a proposal for scrapping preferential policy for FDI was discussed but rejected due to the objection of some key ministries. In July 2005, the RMB was de-pegged and appreciated slightly against the US dollar. Since then the focus of the efforts in rebalancing the international balance of payments has been on reducing trade surplus and capital inflows by ways other than appreciation.

help the poor and disadvantaged. Further liberalization and marketization together with the development of a more extensive social security system will help China achieve a more balanced economy and reduce its chronic current- and capital-account surpluses.

In terms of trade policy, the most consequential change would be reducing or removing tax rebates on exports. Chinese policymakers have long used rebates on exports as a device for promoting industrialization. Those subsidies have been generous, and many enterprises' exports have been aimed at obtaining them. Here then, is another instance where vested interests are likely to resist reform.

Another important measure would be unification of income tax rates on domestic and FFE. In March 2007, the People's Congress passed a resolution to unify the tax rates on Chinese and foreign enterprises. The rate applicable to domestic firms was lowered from 33 to 25 percent, while that applied to FFE was raised from 15/24 percent to 25 percent. It is still too early, however, to know the impact of the convergence of the two tax rates on FDI flows.

Additional policies aiming at reducing the saving-investment gap have or are being adopted. China is in the process of reforming its pension system. Local governments have introduced minimum wage laws. Then, there is the so-called policy of *yanjin kuanchu* ("strict-in, easy-out"), which aims to encourage capital outflows and restrain inflows. As part of this initiative, the category of qualified domestic institutional investors (QDII) was introduced. The aim of QDII is to encourage an orderly outflow of capital. The basic framework for QDII investment includes three types of financial institutions: banks, asset management/securities companies, and insurance companies. Banks apply for a QDII quota from China Banking Regulatory Commission (CBRC). They determine the relevant products and submit them for CBRC approval, within which a maximum 50 percent may be invested in stocks, but only in a foreign market that has signed a memorandum of understanding with CBRC. In the case of asset management companies, approval is on a product-by-product basis by the China Securities Regulatory Commission (CSRC). There is no ceiling on the allocation of investments in stocks and related derivatives, aside from limits on exposure to individual stocks.

At the end of 2006, the total assets of the insurance industry were Rmb 1973 billion, which means that, given the 15 percent rule, Rmb 296 billion could be invested overseas. Most of these investments will likely be in fixed-income and related products, given the structure of the insurance sector's liabilities.

By the end of the first quarter of 2007, the total quota authorized by SAFE under the provisions of this scheme was $18.5 billion. This includes $12.1 billion for Chinese banks, $2.4 billion for foreign banks, $500 million for asset management companies, and $3.5 billion for insurance companies. However, only 5 percent of the total authorized was actually invested abroad by financial institutions in this period.[5] The explanation for this behavior is straightforward: when the renminbi is expected to appreciate, as has been the case for some time, it is not attractive for an institution to accumulate additional foreign-currency-denominated assets.[6]

Even though the central government is trying to scrap preferential treatment of FDI and implement the policy of *yanjin kuachu*, capital inflows have failed to subside — quite to the contrary. Indicative of this is the fact that the errors and omissions in the balance of payments have been strongly positive since 2005. Net capital inflows continue to contribute to the increase in foreign exchange reserves at a rate of $US50–60 billion per annum. (In 2007, they contributed fully $74 billion to foreign exchange reserves.) This increase in capital inflows has two explanations. First, provincial and lower-level governments have resisted the central government's instructions to phase out preferences toward FDI. Second, expectations that the renminbi will continue to appreciate have negated the government's policy of *yanjin kuachu*.

A number of observers have suggested that a substantial portion of the trade surplus is actually disguised speculative capital inflows achieved by over-invoicing exports and under-invoicing imports. The accelerating growth of exports may also reflect enterprises' rush to export before new policies aimed at discouraging exports are implemented, while the sudden appearance of a surplus on investment income is no doubt attributable to expectations of renminbi appreciation. Although there are no reliable statistics on how much of the increase in foreign reserves is attributable to speculative capital inflows, it seems clear that the Chinese government's

---

[5] "Standard Charter: QDII will have its 'beautiful time,'" (Chinese), *The First Financial and Economic Daily*, April 5, 2007.

[6] Another important development is that China Development Bank, a state-owned institution, agreed to invest 2.2 billion euros (roughly $3 billion) in Barclays, the British bank, and to invest an additional 7.6 billion euros if Barclays wins the bidding for ABN Amro (see Credit Suisse Equity Research, 2007).

new trade- and FDI-related policies aimed at reducing the twin surpluses in the balance of payments and slowing the increase in foreign exchange reserves have failed to achieve the desired results.

Managing Foreign Exchange Reserves

The considerable wealth that China has tied up in foreign exchange reserves renders their management increasingly important. Typically, central banks hold foreign exchange reserves in relatively safe, low-yielding US treasury bonds or their equivalent (such as the so-called "agency securities" issued by government-sponsored entities like Freddie Mac and Fannie Mae). Each dollar of reserves that a country invests in these assets comes at an opportunity cost that equals the cost of external borrowing or, alternatively, the social rate of return to investment.

According to a survey by the World Bank of more than 10,000 FFE in China, average profitability is 22 percent.[7] In contrast, the yield on US treasury bills is on the order of 5 percent. This means that the opportunity cost of holding foreign exchange reserves is extremely high (on the order of 17 percent, assuming that these reserves, when invested in productive capacity, could earn the same return as FFE).

This brings us back to the question of why China has accumulated such extensive reserves. Reserves have played multiple roles in the Chinese economy. They are regarded as a store of wealth that can be used in case of emergency or to pay the costs of reforms that cannot be financed via normal fiscal channels; it has been argued, for example, that foreign exchange reserves should be used to finance the expansion of the country's pension system. Reserves have also been used to recapitalize the banking system. In 2004, the PBOC invested $45 billion of foreign exchange reserves in two large state-owned banks, the China Construction Bank (CCB) and the Bank of China (BOC). Then in 2006, $15 billion was injected into the country's largest commercial bank, the Industrial and Commercial Bank of China (ICBC).[8] In the case of CCB and BOC, the

---

[7] Talk on multinationals' profitability in China on 11 November 2006 by World Bank's Country Director for China and Mongolia in the East Asia and Pacific Region, David Dollar. Reported by Xin Hua News Agency on 13 November 2006.

[8] This investment was made via Huijin Investment Company, a financial shareholding company established by the PBOC for the sole purpose of holding the commercial bank shares received in return for the capital injection.

PBOC became the sole owner. In order to prevent the capital injection from causing inflation, the commercial banks were requested by the PBOC to retain the foreign exchange accumulated through these operations and not to convert it into renminbi. However, there were unconfirmed reports that the banks moved at least some of their foreign assets back to China, contributing to capital inflows in the first half of 2007.

Many observers praise the authorities' use of foreign exchange reserves for these purposes because this had the effect of "killing two birds with one stone". It addressed the undercapitalization of the banks while at the same time disposing of excess reserves. That said, the structural problems that caused the banks to get into this mess in the first place and led to the accumulation of such large international reserves have not been addressed. This raises the possibility that the entire process may have to be repeated again in the future at considerable expense to the country and its citizenry.

Until recently, China's SAFE was the sole government body responsible for managing the country's international reserves. State Administration of Foreign Exchange has entire departments responsible for investment decisions. Its traders are experienced professionals. It is said that its internal controls and auditing practices are relatively reliable and developed. Moreover, due to modest salaries, the cost of operating SAFE is low compared with the costs facing other financial institutions active in foreign exchange markets.

Since its establishment some two decades ago, SAFE has performed relatively well. In 2005, its performance was among the best official foreign exchange management institutions according to the results of a survey conducted by the International Monetary Fund (IMF). Its costs were low, and its return on investment was more or less in line with international standards.

In 2000, SAFE formulated plans to diversify its portfolio and improve its risk-return profile. Authorized investments include government bonds, corporate bonds, emerging market bonds, and equities. Geographically, permissible investments cover a wide range of countries and regions. Diversification of investment in terms of currencies is to be done gradually in order not to roil the markets.

Singapore as a Role Model

Notwithstanding this progress, the pressure on the government to increase yields on foreign exchange reserves has continued to grow. For guidance on how to achieve this, the Chinese authorities have looked to the experience of other countries, notably Singapore. The Government of Singapore Investment Corporation Private Limited (GIC) is a global investment management company established by the Government of Singapore in 1981 to manage the government's foreign exchange reserves. Beginning with less than US$6 billion in 1981, GIC has grown substantially. Initially a bondholder, it now invests in equities, fixed income, money market instruments, real estate, commodities, and money markets. The GIC Special Investments manages a diversified global portfolio of investments in venture capital, private equity, and infrastructure. The GIC has invested in 50 hedge funds. It is now placing out a larger proportion of funds to external fund managers.

Over 25 years to March 2006, the rate of return on the foreign reserves managed by GIC averaged 9.5 percent in US dollar terms and 8.2 percent in Singapore dollar terms. The rate of return in real terms (in excess of global inflation) was 5.3 percent. At latest report, half of GIC's portfolio consists of equity investments, while bonds account for 30 percent, and the remainder is made up of private equity, hedge funds, real estate, and commodities.[9] The GIC is also managing part of the reserves of the central bank (the Monetary Authority of Singapore or MAS) on a manager-client basis and earns management fees for its work. The GIC also manages reserves for the Ministry of Finance (MOF). It is incorporated as a self-standing company wholly owned by the government.

In practice, GIC evolved out of the reserve management department of the MAS. As start-up funds, GIC brought with it the assets it had been managing as a straightforward transfer of funds from the MAS. A clear-cut division of labor between GIC and MAS in the management of foreign exchange reserves was established only gradually. In the initial stage, GIC formed a Bond Department to manage the long-term bonds transferred from the MAS. During the early years, GIC obtained many of its officers from the Public Service Commission and the MAS, and a sizeable number continued wearing two hats as officers of both the GIC and MAS. Only in 1987 did GIC move to its own offices at Raffles City Tower where it assumed responsibility for its own corporate functions. By the late 1980s, most of GIC's staff were recruited from the market.

---

[9] Dahinten and Wong (2006).

The relationship among the government, GIC, and the MAS is well defined. The MAS is banker to the government and the agency that intervenes to accumulate foreign exchange by selling Singapore dollars for US dollars in the process of managing the exchange rate. However, the Singapore dollars in MAS are deposited by the government as a result of its budget surpluses. Their conversion to US dollars and other foreign currencies does not change the fact that they continue to belong to the government, and the MAS is merely their custodian. Since most of the money managed by GIC belongs to the government (legally the MOF), GIC reports to the government rather than to the MAS. The point of incorporating GIC as a private company is thus to free it from the constraints of government entities. Among other things, this enables it to pay salaries above civil service levels needed to compete for talent with commercial financial organizations. At a more philosophical level, the separation can be attributed to the view that the MAS, as the central bank, should remain the regulator, while GIC's mandate is to maximize returns from the reserves.

The GIC has only two clients — the Government of Singapore and the MAS. The clients set the investment objectives and monitor the manager's performance. The GIC receives a fee to finance its operating expenditure. The GIC management team runs day-to-day operations and has an autonomy to decide where and how to invest, recruit, and remunerate. In turn, management reports to the Board of Directors, which provides an overall guidance and direction.

The GIC is accountable to its clients, one of which is the government. Correspondingly, GIC comes under the purview of the President of Singapore. The appointment and/or removal of GIC's Directors and the Group Managing Director require the assent of the president. The GIC is also required to submit its financial statements and proposed budget to the president for approval. The president is entitled to request any information from GIC. In addition, GIC is regularly audited by the Auditor General. Even with this oversight, there are controversies over GIC's transparency, which is beyond the scope of this chapter.

Establishment of the State Investment Corporation

There is no disagreement among scholars that a portion of China's reserves should be managed more actively with the goal of achieving higher returns without sacrificing safety. This raises the issue of whether China needs to establish a separate corporation to do this. Many have argued, building on Singapore's experience, that any new entity should be housed in SAFE. Initially, the sections of SAFE that have been in this business for decades should be authorized to more actively manage a portion of the country's international reserves. Eventually, a new corporation analogous to the GIC can be established.

Contrary to this recommendation, the Chinese government has instead opted to create for this purpose a wholly new corporation with no connection to SAFE. The new corporation, the China Investment Corporation (CIC), was established on September 29, 2007. The plan was to recruit staff from the market rather than transferring them from SAFE. The CIC will answer to the state council, and the head of the CIC will be a minister equivalent to the Governor of the POBC and the MOF.

The new corporation's first investment caused a considerable controversy. Even before it was formally founded, CIC struck a deal via an undisclosed entity (reported to have been Huijin Company) with the Blackstone Group, a US private equity fund. The CIC purchased a $3 billion stake in Blackstone and acquired its shares at a discount of just 4.5 percent to the initial offering price. In exchange, the CIC agreed that its shares would have no voting rights and the shares it holds could not be sold for four years.

The deal raised troubling questions (see Fan and Shihau, 2007). What was the CIC's investment strategy? With so many opportunities available, why did it opt for a secretive deal with a US private equity firm? After Blackstone went public in June 2007, its shares fell steeply, pushing down the value of the Chinese government's investment by more than $425 million in just six weeks.[10] China had moved with an unusual speed in agreeing to acquire the Blackstone stake after just a month of negotiation. Why such a rush? There were suggestions that the CIC had been out-maneuvered. As an article published in the *New York Times* put it, "As credit markets deteriorated in June, and as pressure grew in the United States for higher taxes on private equity funds, Blackstone's leaders shrewdly pushed forward the date of the company's initial public offering and priced it at $31 a share, the top of the planned range."[11]

---

[10] See Bradsher (2007).
[11] *Ibid.*

Also controversial was the CIC's funding. In the case of the GIC, the reserves that it manages are owned by the government via the MOF, as noted above, and the question of a transfer of ownership was never raised. The GIC simply acts as a custodian. In China, foreign exchange reserves are owned by the government via the central bank. Evidently, there was a question of how to transfer foreign exchange reserves from the SAFE to a separate entity — the CIC. The government did not want to transfer foreign exchange reserves from the SAFE directly to the CIC, although there was no technical impediment to doing so. As a first step, the MOF therefore issued eight batches of special government bonds to raise funds totaling 1.55 trillion renminbi.[12] A controversial question at the time was to whom these bonds should be sold. The MOF could not sell the bonds directly to the PBOC because doing so was against law. It could not sell the bonds to the public either because of possible negative impacts on the stock exchange.

In the end, the problem was solved by the Agricultural Bank of China (ABC). The MOC sold special government bonds of 1.55 trillion renminbi to the ABC. With the funds thereby raised, it bought $200 billion of foreign exchange from the PBOC, which in turn used the 1.55 trillion renminbi to buy the special government bonds from the ABC. In this way, the MOF obtained the foreign exchange which it then allocated to the CIC. The SAFE ended up with $200 billion fewer in foreign exchange reserves, but the PBOC obtained 155 billion renminbi worth of special government bonds, while nothing changed in the balance sheet of the ABC. The $200 billion worth of foreign exchange constituted the initial balance that CIC was authorized to manage.

According to Li Yong, non-executive director of CIC and the vice minister of finance, one-third of the $200 billion would be used to purchase the Central Huijin Investment Company Limited (Central Huijin) from the PBOC, a second third to inject capital into China Development Bank (CDB) and the ABC, and the remaining third to invest actively in international capital markets.[13] By the end of 2007, the CIC had spent $67 billion to purchase Central Huijin from the PBOC and become the

---

[12] The data is from www.chinabond.com.cn.

[13] "China Investment Corporation Unveils Investment Plan," *China Daily* (12 November 2007), online edition. Central Huijin was established in December 2003 as a vehicle for injecting capital into state-owned commercial banks and securities companies in need of restructuring or seeking to list overseas.

Table 7.1. Overseas investments of the CIC.

Company	Time	Amount (USD)	Type
The Blackstone Group	May 2007	3 bn	Pre-IPO, shares, 9.4% stake
China Railway Group Limited	Nov 2007	100 mn	Pre-IPO, shares
Morgan Stanley	Dec 2007	5 bn	Convertible bond, 9.9% stake, 9% annual return before conversion
VISA	Mar 2008	100 mn	Pre-IPO, shares
JC Flowers PE Fund	Apr 2008	3.2 bn	US PE fund, 80% ownership

Source: SWF institute, FTChinese.com.

sole owner of the company. From May 2007 to the time of writing this Chapter, the CIC has made four share investments directly, and one investment in overseas private equity funds (see Table 7.1). Owing largely to the outbreak of the credit crisis, the market value of several of these investments then declined drastically, arousing strong criticism. In response, the CIC began investing more in domestic markets. This move, however, coincided with a sharp drop in domestic stock markets. In all, the new entity's early experience has been far from smooth.

Should we be concerned about SWF?

In a recent article, the former US Treasury Secretary Lawrence Summers observed that:

> "Inevitably, and appropriately, countries possessed of publicly held foreign assets far in excess of anything needed to respond to financial contingencies feel pressure to deploy them strategically or at least to earn higher returns than those available in US Treasury bills or their foreign equivalents. ... But on any plausible path over the next few years, a crucial question for the global financial system and indeed for the

global economy is how these funds (Sovereign Wealth Funds) will be invested."[14]

Summers called for greater attention to the risks associated with ownership of real assets in the United States by foreign government-controlled entities. The danger he perceived was that SWF might invest strategically with the goal of enhancing the international position of home-country firms, acquiring sensitive foreign technologies, or increasing their government's geopolitical leverage. He went so far as to suggest that SWFs might be able to influence the policy of host governments in undesirable ways.

These fears are almost certainly overdrawn. Summers' worries remind one of the warnings by American commentators in the 1980s about the "invasion" of Japanese investors. China's SWF, in particular, is still at an early stage of development. It will take decades before it accumulates the expertise needed to undertake complex financial transactions and — unlike the case of Blackstone — make money at them. Fears that CIC will exercise leverage over US economic policy seem rather far fetched.

More likely is that in the initial stage, due to lack of experience, China's SWF will book losses on its investments in the United States (as did Japan starting in the late 1980s (Fig. 7.6) and as did the CIC on the Blackstone deal). China's SWF is also likely to outsource the

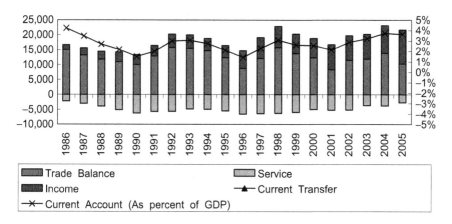

Figure 7.6. Japan's current account (1986–2005) unit: billions yen (left axis).

---

[14] Summers (2007).

management of much of its portfolio to private managers — including US managers. Those managers will invest through US hedge funds and private equity funds, in the manner of US universities investing their endowments. The CIC will no more be able to influence US foreign policy than the Harvard and Yale University endowments. US financial firms, for their part, will earn handsome fees for providing management services.

Conclusion

China's accumulation of foreign reserves, though impressive, is also a problem. Officials are conscious of this and are now implementing policies designed to bring the period of rapid reserve accumulation to a close. They aim to adopt a more market-oriented growth model and to allow the renminbi to appreciate against the dollar, the euro, and the yen.

In line with long-standing Chinese practice, however, it is likely that these new policies will be phased in gradually. By implication, the rate of reserve accumulation will also slow down gradually. This means that the government will continue to face challenges for some time in managing a growing pool of reserves. It will have to diversify its holdings across currencies to attain a better combination of stability and return. And it will want to diversify between debt and equity, which will mean assigning the task of reserve management to portfolio managers independent of the central bank. In other words, a growing share of the country's reserves is likely to come under management by its SWF.

But this should not be a cause for alarm. China is a responsible country. It will not use its sovereign wealth in ways that disrupt international financial markets. Its fundamental interest is in the profitability of its investments. And ensuring profitability, in turn, means contributing to the smooth operation of the markets on which those investments are made.

CHAPTER 8

The Integration Process in East Asia: Japan's Experience and Policy Agenda

Motoshige Itoh

Introduction

For more than a decade, the East Asian economies have been undergoing a process of rapid regional integration. This process includes not just the introduction of free trade agreements (FTAs) and financial-cum-currency cooperation but also increases in private-sector transactions across borders such as trade, foreign direct investment (FDI), portfolio capital flows, and migration. The financial crisis of 1997–98 was a turning point in this process. Before the crisis, governments had been slow to introduce policies promoting regional integration. Subsequently, their efforts intensified and progress has accelerated.

The proliferation of FTAs illustrates the change in policy since the crisis. By the end of the 1990s, only 4 of the largest 30 countries worldwide — all in East Asia — were still not party to an FTA: Japan, China, Korea, and Taiwan. Since the late 1990s, however, this situation has been transformed. The number of FTAs involving East Asian countries has risen rapidly, and the region is now one of the most active in the world in terms of FTA negotiations.

This changing attitude toward regional integration is also evident in the monetary and financial realm. The 1997–98 crisis, in which Asian economies appeared unable to resist the impulses emanating from global financial markets, provided a new impetus for financial cooperation. Although the aspiration to create an Asian Monetary Fund (AMF), mooted by Japan following the outbreak of the crisis, was not realized, the Chiang Mai Initiative (CMI) created a network of bilateral swaps and credits, and the participating countries have taken steps subsequently to augment and multilateralize their arrangement.

The idea of transforming the CMI into a regional monetary fund capable of undertaking lender-of-last-resort operations and supporting the stability of currencies in the region is now under active discussion. Similarly, there has been progress in cultivating a liquid and an active Asian bond market under the aegis of the Asian Bond Fund (ABF) and the Asian Bond Market Initiative (ABMI) of the Executives' Meeting of East Asian-Pacific Central Banks (EMEAP) and ASEAN+3 grouping, respectively.[1]

Many studies and reports have described and analyzed this process from the perspective of the region. This chapter takes a different approach: it describes and analyzes integration-related policies and initiatives from the perspective of an individual country, Japan. Taking the view of a particular country illuminates the process from a different angle. Regional integration involves flows across borders, but it also has implications for the policies and politics of the participating countries. The impact of Asian integration will differ across countries as a function of, inter alia, per capita incomes, stages of economic development, and other national characteristics. Viewing the process from the perspective of a particular country helps to draw out those implications. In addition, the experience of Japan may contain lessons for other Asian economies, as the high incomes, aging population, and other distinctive features of the Japanese case become increasingly prevalent elsewhere in the region.

The Asian Gateway Initiative

In 2007, the Cabinet of then Prime Minister Shinzo Abe launched the Asian Gateway Initiative Council, with the prime minister himself acting as the chairperson. The agenda was to discuss policy measures to further open Japan to neighboring Asian countries and foster the process of regional integration. The creation of this council was indicative of the priority attached by the government to regional integration. Indeed, there has been no other government project in the last 10 years on which the Cabinet Office has focused so intensively.

---

[1] ASEAN+3 referring to the Association of South East Asian Nations plus Japan, China, and South Korea.

Table 8.1 summarizes the policy measures proposed in the report of the Asian Gateway Initiative Council. These cover a wide range of areas, from aviation, financial reform, and customs clearance services to education, agricultural policy reform, and the promotion of Japanese art, culture, and design. One task of the Asian Gateway Initiative is to review domestic policies from the perspective of the regional integration process. In this context, agricultural reform is crucial because a heavily protected agricultural sector constitutes an obstacle to liberalization. Realizing this, the Japanese government is therefore attempting to change its policy stance from the protection of uncompetitive small farmers toward the nurturing of competitive farmers.

The issues enumerated in Table 8.1 are indicative of how domestic structures and regulations continue to throw up obstacles to regional integration. Take, for example, the case of aviation rules. It goes without saying that an efficient aviation network is vital for regional integration: the availability of efficient and flexible aviation services is critical to a wide variety of cross-border economic activities. In North America, where the United States occupies the dominant position, the air transportation industry was substantially deregulated in the late 1970s. In Europe, a "One Sky for Europe" policy has been established. The United States and Europe concluded and implemented the first phase of an open skies agreement in early 2008. Compared to these regions, aviation in East Asia is still highly regulated. Neither Japan nor China has concluded open skies agreements with major partners.[2] Hence, all air traffic to and from the two countries continues to be regulated by bilateral agreements that vary in coverage. Japan does not even have a fully operational 24-hour airport in the Tokyo metropolitan area to act as a regional hub. The Asian Gateway Initiative Council proposal for "Asian Open Skies" is intended to correct this problem. It proposes the creation of a truly free multilateral aviation network in the region.

The second entry in Table 8.1, "Implement a program for streamlining trade measures", similarly illustrates the issues that remain to be

---

[2] Some changes have been observed since the Asian Gateway Initiative was proposed. For example, Japan and Hong Kong reached an agreement to open all their airports (except those in the Tokyo Metropolitan Area). Since this agreement was reached, Hong Kong Express Airline has already opened five routes (between Hong Kong and five cities in Japan).

Table 8.1. Ten major policy priorities under the Asian Gateway Initiative.

1. Change in aviation policy to achieve "Asian Open Skies".

   • Form a strategic international aviation network through aviation liberalization ("Asian Open Skies"); make Haneda Airport more international; facilitate 24-hour operation of major international airports.

2. Implement a program for streamlining trade measures.

   • Reform customs clearance and other relevant procedures to enhance logistical capacity for international trade.

3. Restructure policy regarding foreign students in order for Japan to serve as a hub for a human resource network in Asia.

   • Mobilize stakeholders in order to formulate a new national strategy.

4. Further open up universities to the world.

   • Target educational funds and improve evaluation of universities to encourage their further internationalization.

5. Create financial and capital markets that are attractive to Asian customers.

   • Promote further integration of financial networks in Asia.

6. Transform agriculture into a successful growth industry during an era of globalization.

   • Invigorate agriculture with a focus on entrepreneurial spirit.

7. Create an "Asian Gateway Special Zone".

   • Promote regional exchange in Asia by means of a special zone system for deregulation.

8. Implement policies in line with a comprehensive strategy for "creative industries".

   • Provide a stimulating environment to nurture creative industries and strategically promote them.

9. Promote Japan's attractiveness overseas.

   • Create a Prime Ministerial award to honor those who contribute to the promotion of Japanese design and culture; establish a "Japan Creative Center".

10. Strengthen Japan's central role in promoting regional study and cooperation for solving shared problems.

   • Take the initiative in holding international forums for cooperation in areas such as the environment and energy, as well as establishing a research network.

Source: See text.

addressed before Asia can begin to forge a truly integrated economic zone. Efficient and transparent customs and immigration and quarantine (CIQ) inspections are essential for the speed and security of cross-border trans-actions. Further development of regional supply chains will only be pos-sible if parts and components can move across borders reliably, with a minimum of expense and without delay. Although there have been efforts by Asian countries to upgrade their CIQ systems, progress to date has been spotty. Japan is no exception.

The fifth entry, "Creating financial and capital markets that are attrac-tive to Asian customers", is elaborated further in Table 8.2. The first item there is "disclosure of information in English". It may seem odd that such a simple practice, which is prevalent in virtually all other important trad-ing nations, has not yet been achieved in Japan. Thus, it is not hard to see why international investors continue to participate in Japanese financial markets only to a limited extent given that this basic condition for inter-nationalization has not been met.

Changing Attitudes

Although important issues remain to be resolved, the diplomatic envi-ronment in East Asia has changed drastically since the 1997–98 finan-cial crisis. As noted above, Japan, China, and Korea were not party to any FTAs, and no serious initiatives had been pursued to enhance financial stability at the regional level. Since the crisis, in contrast, there have been myriad economic and financial initiatives to promote regional integration.

What lay behind this change? Certainly, the painful experience of the financial crisis induced governments to think more seriously about regional financial stability. In addition, the facts on the ground — growing amounts of trade and investment and increased financial flows — created a new appreciation of the extent of interdependence and of the need to manage it effectively. These developments raised the question of whether countries would collaborate in developing an environment in which regional public goods would be provided and cross-border activ-ities would flourish or whether they would engage in unhealthy policy competition.

Japan's trade with East Asian countries expanded rapidly in the 1990s. By mid-decade, trade with East Asia was as important as trade

Table 8.2. Ten reform proposals for financial and capital markets under the Asian Gateway Initiative.

1. Establish a system to provide funds for growth to Asia.
   * Include the disclosure of information in English.
2. Build a globally competitive financial capital market infrastructure and other systems.
   * Include the establishment of a centralized clearing system to handle the settlement of funds and securities.
3. Create a professional financial market and foster financial professionals.
   * Include the establishment of a trading venue for and between professionals and the promotion of deregulation in disclosure of information in English, the taxation system, and standards of disclosure.
4. Improve access to Japanese markets as international financial centers.
   * Include the facilitation of 24-hour operation of major international airports and promotion of aviation liberalization.
5. Improve financial regulation and administration systems and increase their transparency.
   * Enhance the functions of genuine self-regulatory organizations.
   * Formulate a clear definition of the financial and capital market rules and an objective standard of behavior for the competent authorities.
6. Eliminate barriers that block the flow of funds within the Asian region.
   * Aggressively promote financial services deregulation at Economic Partnership Agreement (EPA) negotiations and other talks.
7. Enhance regional financial cooperation that goes beyond the CMI.
   * Promote the multilateralization of the CMI.
8. Create a cross-border international bond market in Asia.
9. Build a common financial platform for Asian countries.
   * Enhance intellectual and technical support for the improvement of Asian markets, based on Japan's experience in financial reforms.
10. Implement required policies in Japan in approximately three years in a focused manner.
    * In particular, implement policies related to the disclosure of information in English within a year.

Source: See text.

with the United States and Europe combined. Trade with China (inclusive of Hong Kong) exceeded trade with the United States in 2007. Japan's trade with Asia is disproportionately comprised of intermediate goods. This is indicative of an extensive cross-border division of labor and the articulation of regional production networks. Additionally, diverse economic conditions among countries in the region in terms of wages and technological sophistication make it possible for firms to enjoy the benefits of an extensive cross-border division of labor. The industries involved are numerous, but notable examples include motor vehicles, electronics and electrical machinery, all sectors in which Japanese firms have considerable presence.

It was this market-led integration of production and investment and not political negotiations that initially propelled the process of East Asian regionalism. In Europe and North America, diplomatic efforts came first, or at least developed concurrently, with the deepening of investment and production linkages. In East Asia, the sequencing was the reverse. With time, economic integration then provided further impetus for political initiatives. A growing cross-border division of labor motivated firms to seek lower trade barriers so that they could incorporate more countries in their production networks. Their lobbying has made governments aware that economic integration is valued by their constituents. Japanese firms have established production networks throughout ASEAN countries, and they are increasingly pressing for the reduction of barriers at and behind the border.

As recently as a decade ago, FTA negotiations had only a secondary position in the rank order of policies in Japan. This neglect of FTA policies was symbolized by the fact that they were delegated to individual ministries; no effort was made by the prime minister's office to coordinate the overall negotiation. One ASEAN negotiator likened the situation to "negotiating with different countries" depending on the producer or sector under discussion; he referred to multiple Japans — "the agriculture country", "the labor country", "the industry country", and so on — reflecting the absence of interministerial coordination.[3] This situation caused frustration and slowed progress.

Leadership by the prime minister is vital for the successful negotiation of any FTA, given that different ministries have different priorities and views of the desirability of an agreement. For example, in Japan, the agricultural sector has strongly opposed liberalization and its views inform the position of the ministry. It is not easy for other ministries to

---

[3] This is based on a private conversation with a trade official from an ASEAN country.

persuade it to liberalize the market without the strong leadership from the prime minister.[4]

One factor encouraging Japan to revise its approach to FTAs is the proliferation of bilateral FTAs among neighboring countries such as China and South Korea. Another is the initiative from the Association of South East Asian Nations to create an ASEAN economic community within which merchandise and (within limits) factors of production will be free to move.[5] When Japan negotiated its first FTA with Singapore, China and Korea were not yet negotiating FTAs of their own; thus, the negotiations with Singapore proceeded without a sense of urgency. But then the entry of China and Korea into the FTA arena transformed the outlook of Japanese officials, who came to believe that failing to conclude further FTA negotiations in short order might cause Japan to be left behind. As Asia proceeded with the creation of an integrated economic zone, Japan worried that it would find itself isolated economically and diminished in diplomatic influence.

The increasing number of FTAs being concluded not only by neighboring countries but also in other parts of the world has worked in the same direction. Given the preferences enjoyed by firms from the signatory countries, failure to participate in analogous FTA negotiations would put Japanese firms at a disadvantage in overseas markets. Mexico is a good example: that country has been aggressively engaged in FTA negotiations with numerous countries, among them the United States, Canada, and the European Union (EU). Products from the United States and EU are now free of duty when entering the Mexican market, while Japanese products continue to face high tariffs. The Japanese business community as well as the Ministry of Economy, Trade and Industry have been particularly concerned about this kind of discrimination, which has induced them to come out strongly in favor of FTAs.[6]

By the end the Koizumi government (2001–2006), FTAs had become a higher priority for the cabinet. The plan for 2006 included concrete schedules for FTA negotiations with ASEAN countries. India, the Gulf Cooperation

---

[4] When Japan opened its domestic rice market following the Uruguay Round agreement, the government offered a significant amount of subsidies to the agricultural sector. This kind of compensation by subsidies is now more difficult to implement due to the present budget deficit problem.

[5] The putative deadline for completion of the ASEAN economic community is 2015.

[6] The Japanese government initiated and speeded up FTA negotiations with Mexico and could finish the negotiation in a short period.

Council (GCC) countries, Chile, and Australia were also included in the list of possible partners. In addition, the government developed a plan for negotiating a region-wide network of FTAs encompassing ASEAN+3 countries or ASEAN+3 together with India, Australia, and New Zealand. The subsequent Abe cabinet placed an even stronger emphasis on regional integration policy. The Economic and Fiscal Council, the government's most important economic-policy body, formed a project team chaired by the prime minister to accelerate FTA negotiations. The Prime Minister's Office also established another special project team, the Asian Gateway Initiative Council (as described above), to discuss the potential for accelerating negotiations with neighboring countries.

Singapore was Japan's first partner in FTA negotiations, as noted.[7] Thailand, Malaysia, the Philippines, and Indonesia were then targeted as its successors. But despite the high volume of Northeast Asian trade, the Japanese made no serious moves to initiate FTA negotiations with China. In the case of Korea, FTA negotiations have stalled: there has been no follow-up to the joint Japan–Korea study group that reported in 2002, and no serious efforts have been taken on the Japanese side to restart them.

Why this lack of urgency in negotiating agreements with China and Korea? The Japanese government considers the ASEAN region as critical to Japan's economic and political security. The country's stock of foreign investments in this region is larger than its investment in China and Korea. It also has provided a significant amount of official development aid to its ASEAN partners. Supporting the stability, growth and integration of the ASEAN countries has been a policy priority for Japan since the Asian currency crisis. Successive governments have made a variety of efforts to promote currency cooperation; some, such as the proposal to establish an AMF, have not been realized, but others, such as negotiating a network of bilateral swaps and credits, nurturing Asian bond markets, and establishing an Asian currency unit (ACU), have borne fruit.

It is relevant in this context to note that there were debates in the government several years ago over the choice between two different approaches

---

[7] There is a saying in Japan, "it is best for a baby to be small while being carried by its mother, and to become bigger after he/she is born". One of the reasons why Singapore was chosen as Japan's first partner in FTA negotiations was the small scale of its economy.

toward negotiating FTAs with the ASEAN countries, one of which was to negotiate individually with each ASEAN country, the other being to negotiate with ASEAN as a group. Korea, China, and Australia have adopted the latter approach, while Japan has pursued the two approaches in parallel. Time will tell which of the two approaches is more productive.

Domestic Issues as an Obstacle to Regional Free Trade

It is widely believed that opposition from Japan's agricultural sector poses the most serious obstacle to any liberalization policy, including FTAs. Japanese farmers have always opposed liberalization of the agricultural sector, and their political influence has slowed the progress of both GATT/WTO negotiations and FTA negotiations. But several factors have contributed to the decline of the agricultural lobby's political influence. Japan's farmers are rapidly aging as a group; their average age is 65. The share of the agricultural sector is continuing to fall due to the evolution toward a more manufacturing- and service-based economy.

Although this declining sector may retain excessive political influence, the phenomenon is not limited to Japan. The textile and automotive industries in the United States, also arguably in decline, retain strong political influence despite falling market share. This reflects the concentrated nature of the interest, which gives employers and workers the incentive and ability to engage in political action; while consumers, whose interests are diffuse, do not have similar incentive to lobby for their interests.

At the same time, political reforms have worked to tip the balance of power and influence in new directions. Changes such as the single-seat electoral district system brought about changes in decision making and in the balance of political power. A single-seat system does not allow a particular lobbying group such as farmers to keep strong influence, since their power is now fragmented among many small electoral districts. The result has been to make it more difficult for small groups to control political decisions through elections. Illustrative of this fact, vested interests did not succeed in preventing the privatization of postal savings under the Koizumi Government.[8]

Japan's agricultural industry has been characterized by a preponderance of farmers with very small holdings who obtained their farmland at the time of the land reform policy after World War II.[9] Smallholdings of this sort tend to be relatively inefficient since they do not allow farmers to enjoy large-scale production of such products as rice and wheat, and the government adopted various measures to support their proprietors. Now these farmers are very old. From the viewpoint of the efficient use of agricultural land, the farmland owned by these aging small farmers should be consolidated under new ownership. Demands are increasingly heard for the introduction of policies to promote competition in the agricultural sector: for shifts from protecting small farmers to supporting competitive farmers and new styles of management for farming activities, and from import restriction to the promotion of production. Some farmers, seeing the writing on the wall, have embraced these changes rather than resisted them. It is too early to say whether these developments will change Japan's agricultural trade policy, but there are grounds for hope.

More broadly, Japan's FTA negotiations have changed public perceptions of these and other economic policies. In the absence of trade negotiations, ordinary citizens would not have been aware of the extent of agricultural protection. Similarly, FTA negotiations with Mexico revealed the extent of measures limiting imports of pork and those with Thailand policies preventing imports of chicken. Likewise, the resistance of the Japan Nurses Association to negotiations with the Philippines concerning immigration of medical workers revealed to the public the self-interested actions of that organization. Once the influence of special-interest groups

---

[8] In Japan, this phenomenon is often linked with the unique character of former Prime Minister Koizumi. Although Mr. Koizumi played an important role in changing the political scene in Japan, many political scientists point out that the changing structure of Japanese politics cannot be attributed only to Mr. Koizumi's personal character, but should be understood as a more fundamental change occurring in recent years.

[9] In order to support small farmers, the government did not allow corporate involvement in agricultural activities. Deregulation regarding this issue is now being discussed by the government.

such as farmers and the Nurses Association became known, politicians representing the general interest called for those groups to be less aggressive in opposing liberalization.

Thus, one of the most important motives for pursuing FTA policies is to promote domestic reform. It is not easy to change a political system from within. Existing systems have been built on a balance of countervailing forces, and this kind of political equilibrium is difficult to disturb from inside.[10] Hence, FTA policies are useful not only for enabling improved trade access but also for promoting domestic reforms. Sectors such as agriculture, education, medical services, and retail can be transformed by exposing them to international competition.

Toward Enhanced Monetary and Financial Cooperation

It may be illuminating to apply the above framework to the issue of monetary and financial cooperation. The following question can be posed: "Why should the countries of East Asia engage in efforts toward financial and currency cooperation?" To answer this, we must first define monetary cooperation or integration. In the East Asian context, cooperation is composed of four elements. First, a cooperative exchange-rate arrangement is needed, conceivably leading in the long run to the creation of a single regional currency. Second, macroeconomic policy coordination should be based on the adoption of harmonized inflation targets. Third, a common currency basket (an ACU) should be used for cross-border transactions within the region. And, fourth, existing schemes such as increasing the use of Asian bonds, extending currency swaps, and providing funds for currency intervention need to be strengthened.

As discussed at the outset of this chapter, East Asia has not yet established a formal framework for regional integration. Although a network of FTAs has been built, Japan, China, and Korea, which are responsible for a large amount of trade and investment in the region, have not yet concluded

---

[10] The so-called *gaiatsu* (foreign pressure) is well known from the literature regarding trade conflicts between Japan and the United States. *Gaiatsu* has been quite effective in changing domestic regulations in Japan. It is often said that the effectiveness of *gaiatsu* shows Japan's lack of ability to reform itself from inside. However, this is a rather naïve view.

FTAs among themselves. Neither have the countries of the region negotiated meaningful investment treaties, nor have they reached an agreement for the governance of migration. There also has been little progress in the mutual recognition of standards and licenses, in the harmonization of aviation rules, or in deregulating cross-border financial transactions. It will be impossible to move further in the direction of monetary integration without progress in these areas, since further integration of product and factor markets is a prerequisite for monetary harmonization. It is revealing that the countries of Western Europe had to first complete their single market before moving ahead with the creation of the euro.

An intermediate step would be to attempt to stabilize East Asian exchange rates against one another while the region's single market is being completed, again following the example of Europe, which created a multilateral system of pegs — the European Monetary System (EMS) — well before its single market was complete. Currency pegs are not unfamiliar in Asia. Many countries pegged their exchange rates to the dollar prior to the Asian financial crisis, where pegging to the dollar was an indirect way of stabilizing Asian currencies against one another. But the experience of the crisis rightly cast doubt on the feasibility and desirability of soft pegs in an environment of high capital mobility like that which increasingly characterizes the East Asia region. Pegs are hard to defend in a world of liquid financial markets. If not accompanied by prudential supervision and effective corporate governance, they can encourage reckless, unhedged borrowing and lending. They hamstring economic management in that central banks lose their monetary independence.[11] In effect, Asian countries pegging to the dollar delegate their monetary policies to the Federal Reserve Board, which does not create and manage such policies with Asian conditions in mind. Pegging to one another, through an Asian analog to the EMS, would create the same tensions, albeit in a somewhat different form.

Although currency unification or any kind of pegging system may be inconceivable for the near future, it should be possible for the region to achieve a modicum of exchange-rate stability by coordinating monetary policies. If all countries adopted a similar monetary stance, for example

---

[11] This is the implication of the so-called "trilemma" of international macroeconomics — that a country cannot at the same time have three things: open capital markets, a pegged exchange rate, and an independent monetary policy.

by adopting similar inflation targets, the exchange rates between their currencies would tend to settle down.[12] To this end, it would be useful to intensify macroeconomic policy dialog and search for a mechanism for policy coordination. It would be not easy to move directly to a formal scheme such as coordinated inflation targeting, but it should be possible to agree on an incremental approach.

Creating a basket-based currency unit — the ACU — as a unit of account for international transactions in the region, as advocated inter alia by the Asian Development Bank (ADB), would be a useful step. But this initiative would bring about a significant reduction in exchange risk and in the disruptions caused by exchange-rate fluctuations only if the unit is actively used in cross-border transactions. And this would not occur automatically; adoption, given the advantages of the incumbent national currencies, would require an active government support.

An AMF, as proposed in 1997 by Japanese government, could also help to promote the coordination of macroeconomic policies in addition to serving as an exchange-rate stabilizer. Consider the role played by the IMF. In its early stage, the IMF supported the stability of exchange rates with funds subscribed by the governments of member countries. The role of the IMF changed in 1973, when major countries shifted to flexible exchange rates, to one that supports financial stabilization, primarily in developing countries.

During the Asian financial crisis, the countries in the region had difficulty with the IMF's conditionality. They were asked to raise interest rates and restrict fiscal expenditures amid very weak economic conditions. The perception was that these conditions were too demanding and prescriptive and that they were insensitive to both financial and political circumstances in Asia.

Under the circumstances, it was natural for Asian countries to consider establishing their own institutional framework for financial stabilization. Although the original proposal for the AMF was torpedoed by the negative reaction of the United States and the skeptical attitude of China, ongoing efforts to promote financial cooperation in the region may lead to the re-emergence of the concept.

The role played by the AMF will be different from that of the early IMF. The objective of the IMF at the outset was to support the pegged but

---

[12] For more discussion of this point, see the Chapter 2 by Eichengreen in this volume.

adjustable dollar-linked exchange rates of the Bretton Woods System. It would be unwise to attempt to recreate a Bretton Woods-style system in Asia, given the reality of open capital markets. (Recall that the original Bretton Woods System functioned in a world of pervasive capital controls, as did the EMS in the 1980s.) But the funds of the AMF could still be deployed to enable central banks to engage in stabilizing intervention when currency-market conditions threatened to become disorderly. In addition, the AMF could become an important arena for discussing regional macroeconomic policy coordination and an institution for the firm surveillance of macroeconomic policies in the region.

Conclusion

The interdependence of the countries and economies of East Asia applies pressure to those responsible for formulating domestic policies to move away from an inner-looking system toward a more open system. This is already true of trade, a fact that has led to the integration of production and investment in the region and begun to precipitate important policy reforms. The negotiation of FTAs has further encouraged that integration and intensified the pressure for reform. Moving further in the direction of monetary and financial integration will ratchet up this pressure. Ultimately, the benefits for Asia will include not just more efficient and globally competitive economies as regional supply chains and production networks continue to expand but also a more effective set of policies as the pressure for reform is felt.

References

Adams, Charles and Hwee Kwan Chow (2007). "Asian Currency Baskets: A Useful Surveillance Tool?" <https://zeus.econ.umd.edu/cgi-bin/conference/download.cgi?db_name=FEMES07&paper_id=197>.

Adams, Timothy D (2006). "Remarks at the World Economic Forum-East Asia Panel on Asia's Financial Integration: A Miracle in the Making?" U.S. Treasury (June), Washington, D.C.

Aggarwala, Ramgopal (2003). "Road to a Single Currency for South Asia." *RIS Policy Brief* 9 (December): 1–4.

Anderson, Jonathan (2006). "Still Not a Great Idea." UBS Investment Research: Asia Focus (May 12), UBS Securities Asia, Ltd.

Aslund, Anders (2007). *Russia's Capitalist Revolution: Why Market Reform Succeeded and Democracy Failed.* Washington, D.C.: Peterson Institute for International Economics.

Bernanke, Ben, Thomas Laubach, Frederic Mishkin, and Adam Posen (1999). *Inflation Targeting: Lessons from the International Experience.* Princeton, N.J.: Princeton University Press.

Bird, Graham and Ramkishen S. Rajan (2002). "The Evolving Asian Financial Architecture," *Essays in International Economics* 226(February): 1–60. International Economics Section, Princeton University.

Bradsher, Keith (2007). "Feeling the Heat, Not Breathing Fire." *New York Times*, 2 August.

Chai, Hee-Yul and Yeongseop Rhee (2005). "Alternatives of Cross-Border Securities Settlement System in East Asia." *Journal of International Economic Studies* 9(2): 1–35.

Chai, Hee-Yul and Deok Ryong Yoon (2007). "Post-CMI, Financial Market Development, and the RCU: Connections between Financial Cooperation and Monetary Cooperation Initiatives." Paper presented to the conference on "Options for Monetary and Exchange Rate Cooperation in Asia" organized by the North-East Asia Research Foundation (EAMC Forum), Seoul, 23 August 2007.

Cheung, Yin-Wong and Jude Yuen (2003). "A Currency Union in Asia: An Output Perspective." Paper presented to the CESifo Venice Summer Institute Workshop on Monetary Unions after EMU, 21–22 July.

China Economic Net (2007). "ASEAN Plus Three Proposes Pooling Reserves of Members to Curb Currency Volatility." (4 May) <en.ce.cn.org>.

Choi, Gongpil (2007). "Toward an Exchange Rate Mechanism for Emerging Asia." In Duck-Koo Chung and Barry Eichengreen (eds.), *Toward an East Asian Exchange Rate Regime* 121–136. Washington, D.C.: Brookings Institution.

Cooper, Richard (1971). "Currency Devaluation in Developing Countries." *Princeton Essays in International Finance* 86 (June).

Cowen, David, Ranil Sagado, Hemant Shah, Leslie Teo and Alessandro Zanello (2006). "Financial Integration in Asia: Recent Developments and Next Steps," IMF Working Paper No. WP/06/196 (August).

Credit Suisse Equity Research (2007). "More Psychological Than Real Impact — At Least in Near-Term." Zurich: Credit Suisse Group, 26 July.

Crowther, Geoffrey (1957). *Balances and Imbalances of Payments*. Cambridge, Massachusetts: Harvard University Press.

Dahinten, Jan and Fayen Wong (2006). "Singapore's GIC to Invest More in High-Risk Assets," Singapore: Reuters, 11 July.

Dammers, Clifford and Robert N. McCauley (2006). "Basket Weaving: The Euromarket Experience with Basket Currency Bonds." *BIS Quarterly Review* (March): 79–92.

De Brouwer, Gordon and Yunjong Wang (2003). "Policy Dialogue, Surveillance and Financial Cooperation in East Asia." In Gordon de Brouwer and Yunjong Wang (eds.), *Financial Governance in East Asia* 1–15. London: Routledge-Curzon.

De Grauwe, Paul and Francesco Paalo Mongelli (2005). "Endogeneities of Optimum Currency Areas: What Brings Countries Sharing a Single Currency Closer Together?" European Central Bank Working Paper No. 468 (April).

Di Nicolo, Gianni, Patrick Honohan, and Alain Ize (2003). "Dollarization of the Banking System: Good or Bad?" IMF Working Paper No. WP/03/146 (July).

Dowd, Kevin and David Greenaway (1993). "Currency Competition, Network Externalities and Switching Costs: Towards an Alternative View of Optimum Currency Areas." *Economic Journal* 103(420): 1180–1189.

Eichengreen, Barry (1996). *Globalizing Capital: A History of the International Monetary System*. Princeton, N.J.: Princeton University Press.

Eichengreen, Barry (2006). "The Parallel Currency Approach to Asian Monetary Integration." *American Economic Association Papers and Proceedings* 96(2): 432–436.

Eichengreen, Barry (2007a). *The European Economy Since 1945*. Princeton, N.J.: Princeton University Press.

Eichengreen, Barry (2007b). "The Role of the Exchange Rate in Inflation Targeting: The Case of Korea." In Nicoletta Batini (ed.), *Monetary Policy in*

Emerging Markets and Other Developing Countries 117–140. New York: Nova.

Eichengreen, Barry (2007c). "Parallel Processes? Monetary Integration in Europe and Asia." In Duck-Koo Chung and Barry Eichengreen (eds.), *Toward an East Asian Exchange Rate Regime* 137–156. Washington D.C.: Brookings Institution Press.

Eichengreen, Barry and Tamim Bayoumi (1999). "Is Asia an Optimal Currency Area? Can It Become One?" In Stefan Collignon, Jean Pisani-Ferry, and Yung Chul Park (eds.), *Exchange Rate Policies in Emerging Asian Countries* 3–34. London: Routledge.

Eichengreen, Barry and Alan Taylor (2004). "The Monetary Consequences of a Free Trade Area of the Americas." In Antoni Estevadeordal, Dani Rodrik, Alan Taylor and Andres Velasco (eds.), *Integrating the Americas: FTAA and Beyond* 189–226. Cambridge, MA: Rockefeller Center for Latin American Studies, Harvard University.

Feldstein, Martin S. (1983). "Domestic Saving and International Capital Movements in the Long Run and the Short Run." *European Economic Review* 21(1–2): 129–151.

Feldstein, Martin S. (1998). "Refocusing the IMF," *Foreign Affairs* 77: 20–33.

Fischer, Stanley, Richard Cooper, Rudiger Dornbusch, Peter Garber, Carlos Massad, Jacques Polak, Dani Rodrik, and Savak Tarapore. 1998. "Should the IMF Pursue Capital Account Convertibility?" *Princeton Essays in International Finance* 207: 1–10.

Frankel, Jeffrey A. (2005). "Contractionary Currency Crashes in Developing Countries." *IMF Staff Papers* 52: 149–192.

Frankel, Jeffrey Alexander and Andrew K. Rose (1998). "The Endogeneity of the Optimum Currency Area Criteria." *Economic Journal* 108(449): 1009–1025.

Genberg, Hans (2006). "Exchange-Rate Arrangements and Financial Integration in East Asia: On a Collision Course?" Hong Kong Institute for Monetary Research Working Paper No. 15 (November).

Giovannini, Alberto (1989). "How Do Fixed Exchange Rate Regimes Work?" In Marcus Miller, Barry Eichengreen, and Richard Portes (eds.), *Blueprints for Exchange Rate Management* 13–43. New York: Basic Books.

Giovannini Group (2001). "Cross-Border Clearing and Settlement Arrangements in the European Union." Brussels: European Commission.

Giovannini Group (2003). "Second Report on EU Clearing and Settlement Arrangements." Brussels: European Commission.

Giovanoli, Mario (1989). "The Role of the Bank for International Settlements in International Monetary Cooperation and Its Tasks Relating to the European Currency Unit." *The International Lawyer* 23(4): 841–864.

Girardin, Eric (2004). "Information Exchange, Surveillance Systems and Regional Institutions in East Asia." In Asian Development Bank (ed.),

Monetary and Financial Integration in East Asia: The Way Ahead, Volume 1, 53–95. Houndmills and New York: Palgrave Macmillan.

Girardin, Eric and Alfred Steinherr (2008). "Regional Monetary Units for East Asia: Lessons from Europe." ADBI Discussion Paper No. 116 (September), Asian Development Bank Institute, Tokyo.

Goodfriend, Marvin and Eswar Prasad (2006). "Monetary Policy Implementation in China." In Hans Genberg and Eli Remolona (eds.), *Monetary Policy in Asia: Approaches and Implementation, BIS Papers* No. 31 (December), 25–39. Basel, Switzerland: Bank for International Settlements.

Grice, Joe (1990). "The UK Proposals for a European Monetary Fund and a 'Hard ECU': Making Progress Towards Economic and Monetary Union in Europe." *HM Treasury Bulletin* (October): 1–9.

Gros, Daniel and Niels Thygesen (1999). *European Monetary Integration, 2nd Edition.* Harlow: Pearson/Longman Publishing Group.

Gupta, Abhijit Sen and Amitendu Palit (2008). "Feasibility of an Asian Currency Unit." Working Paper No. 208 (March), Indian Council for Research on International Economic Relations, New Delhi.

Hamada, Koichi (2006). "A Remark on the Political Economy of East Asia." Paper presented to the Young Leaders Forum 2006 "East Asian Integration" organized by Japanese-German Center Berlin (JDZB), Reichenow, August.

Honohan, Patrick and Philip R. Lane (1999). "Pegging to the Dollar and the Euro." *International Finance* 2(3): 379–410.

Ito, Takatoshi, Eiji Ogawa and Yuri Sasaki (1998). "How Did the Dollar Peg Fall in Asia?" *Journal of the Japanese and International Economies* 12(4): 256–304.

Ito, Takatoshi and Yung Chul Park (eds.) (2004). *Developing Asian Bond Markets.* Canberra: Asia Pacific Press.

Kawai, Masahiro (2002). "Exchange Rate Arrangements in East Asia: Lessons from the 1997–98 Currency Crisis." *Monetary and Economic Studies* 20 (No. S-1 Special Edition): 167–204.

Kawai, Masahiro (2005). "East Asian Economic Regionalism: Progress and Challenges." *Journal of Asian Economics* 16(1): 29–55.

Kawai, Masahiro (2006). "Creating an Asian Currency Unit." *Japan Journal* 3(5) (September): 10–12.

Kawai, Masahiro (2007a). "Toward a Regional Exchange Rate Regime in East Asia." ADB Institute Discussion Paper No. 68 (June).

Kawai, Masahiro (2007b). "Emerging Asian Regionalism: Ten Years after the Crisis." Comments at the ADB Institute's Study Finalization Workshop, 1–2 November.

Kawai, Masahiro and Cindy Houser (2008). "Evolving ASEAN+3 ERPD: Towards Peer Reviews or Due Diligence?" In Organisation for Economic Co-operation and Development (ed.), *Shaping Policy Reform and Peer Review in Southeast Asia: Integrating Economies and Diversity* 65–98. Paris: OECD.

Kawai, Masahiro and Shinji Takagi (2005a). "Strategy for a Regional Exchange Rate Arrangement in East Asia: Analysis, Review and Proposal." *Global Economic Review* 34(1) (March): 21–64.

Kawai, Masahiro and Shinji Takagi (2005b). "Towards Regional Monetary Cooperation in East Asia: Lessons from Other Parts of the World." *International Journal of Finance and Economics* 10(April): 97–116.

Kawai, Masahiro and Ganeshan Wignaraja (2008). "EAFTA or CEPEA: What Makes Sense?" Forthcoming in *ASEAN Economic Bulletin*.

Kenen, Peter B. (1969). "The Theory of Optimum Currency Areas: An Eclectic View." In Robert Alexander Mundell and Alexander. K. Swoboda (eds.), *Monetary Problems of the International Economy*, 41–60. Chicago: University of Chicago Press.

Kim, Bonghan and Jeong Seeun (2007). "Relative Effects of the Dollar and Yen on East Asian Currency Values: Focusing on the Post-Crisis Period." *Journal of International Economic Studies* 11(1): 119–156.

Krugman, Paul (1991). "Target Zones and Exchange Rate Dynamics." *Quarterly Journal of Economics* 106(3): 669–682.

Kuroda, Haruhiko (2006). "Towards Deeper Asian Economic Integration: Progress and Prospects." Keynote address at the Asia Business Conference, Harvard University Business School, Cambridge, MA, 11 February.

Kuroda, Haruhiko and Masahiro Kawai (2002). "Strengthening Regional Financial Cooperation in East Asia." *Pacific Economic Papers* 51 (October): 1–45.

Kuttner, Kenneth and Adam Posen (2001). "Beyond Bipolar: A Three-Dimensional Assessment of Monetary Frameworks." *International Journal of Finance and Economics* 6(4): 369–387.

Kwan, Chi Hung (2001). *Yen Bloc — Toward Economic Integration in Asia.* Washington, D.C.: Brookings Institution.

Leiderman, Leonardo and Hadas Bar-Or (2002). "Monetary Policy Rules and Transmission Mechanisms under Inflation Targeting in Israel." In Norman Loayza and Klaus Schmidt-Hebbel (eds.), *Monetary Policy: Rules and Transmission Mechanisms*, Series on Central Banking, Analysis and Economic Policies, Volume 4, 393–425. Santiago: Central Bank of Chile.

Ludlow, Peter (1982). *The Making of the European Monetary System.* London: Butterworths.

Ma, Guonan and Robert N. McCauley (2007). "Do China's Capital Control Still Bind? Implication for Monetary Autonomy and Capital Liberalization." *BIS Working Papers* No. 233 (August).

Manupipatpong, Worapot (2002). "The ASEAN Surveillance Process and the East Asian Monetary Fund." *ASEAN Economic Bulletin* 19(April): 111–122.

Manzano, George (2001). "Is There Any Value-Added in the ASEAN Surveillance Process?" *ASEAN Economic Bulletin* 18(April): 94–102.

McKinnon, Ronald Ian (1963). "Optimum Currency Areas." *American Economic Review* 53(4): 717–725.

McKinnon, Ronald I. (1998). "Exchange Rate Coordination for Surmounting the East Asian Currency Crisis." *Asian Economic Journal* 12(4): 317–329.

Mishkin, Frederic and Klaus Schmidt-Hebbel (2001). "One Decade of Inflation Targeting in the World: What Do We Know and What Do We Need to Know?" NBER Working Paper No. 8397 (July).

Mohanty, Madhusudan and Phillip Turner (2005). "Interventions: What Are the Domestic Consequences?" In Bank for International Settlements (ed.) *Foreign Exchange Market Intervention in Emerging Markets: Motives, Techniques and Implications* 56–81. Basel: BIS.

Montiel, Peter J. (2004). "An Overview of Monetary and Financial Integration in East Asia." In Asian Development Bank (ed.), *Monetary and Financial Integration in East Asia: The Way Ahead,* Volume 1, 1–52. Houndmills and New York: Palgrave Macmillan.

Moon, Woosik and Yeongseop Rhee (2006). "Spot and Forward Market Intervention Operations During the 1997 Korean Currency Crisis." *Banca Nazionale del Lavaro Quarterly Review* 59 (September) (238): 243–268.

Moon, Woosik and Yeongseop Rhee (2007). "Financial Integration and Exchange Rate Coordination in East Asia." Paper presented to the conference on "Options for Monetary and Exchange Rate Cooperation in Asia" organized by the North-East Asia Research Foundation (NEAR Forum), Seoul, 23 August.

Moon, Woosik, Yeongseop Rhee and Deokryong Yoon (2000). "Asian Monetary Cooperation: A Search for Regional Monetary Stability in the Post-Euro and the Post-Asian Crisis Era." *Economic Papers* 3(1): 159–193.

Mori, Junichi, Maoyoshi Kinukawa, Hideki Nukaya, and Masashi Hashimoto (2002). "Integration of East Asian Economics and a Step-by-Step Approach Towards a Currency Basket Regime." Institute for International Monetary Affairs Research Report No. 2 (November).

Mundell, Robert Alexander (1961). "A Theory of Optimum Currency Areas." *American Economic Review* 51(4): 657–665.

Mundell, Robert A. (2002). "Does Asia Need a Common Currency Market?" *Pacific Economic Review* 7(1): 3–12.

Ogawa, Eiji and Takatoshi Ito (2002). "On the Desirability of a Regional Basket Currency Arrangement." *Journal of the Japanese and International Economies* 16: 317–334.

Ogawa, Eiji and Junko Shimizu (2005). "A Deviation Measurement for Coordinated Exchange Rate Policies in East Asia." Research Institute of Economy, Trade and Industry (RIETI) Discussion Paper Series 05-E-017 (May).

Ogawa, Eiji and Junko Shimizu (2006). "AMU Deviation Indicator for Coordinated Exchange Rate Policies in East Asia and its Relation with Effective Exchange Rates." *The World Economy* 29(12): 1691–1708.

Park, Yung-Chul, and Doo-Yong Yang (2006). "Prospects for Regional Financial and Monetary Integration in East Asia." Policy References no. 06-06, Seoul: Korea Institute for International Economic Policy (October).

Rajan, Ramkishen and Reza Siregar (2004). "Centralized Reserve Pooling for the ASEAN+3 Countries." In Asian Development Bank (ed.), *Monetary and Financial Integration in East Asia: The Way Ahead,* Volume 2, 285–329. Houndmills and New York: Palgrave Macmillan.

Reinhart, Carmen, Kenneth Rogoff and Miguel Savastano (2003). "Addicted to Dollars." NBER Working Paper No. 10015 (October).

Research Institute of Economy, Trade and Industry (RIETI) (2006). "AMU and AMU Derivation Indicators." <http://www.rieti.go.jp/users/amu/en/detail.html>.

Rodrik, Dani (2006). "The Social Cost of Foreign Exchange Reserves." NBER Working Paper no. 11952 (January).

Rose, Andrew (2006). "A Stable International Monetary System Emerges: Inflation Targeting is Bretton Woods Reversed." NBER Working Paper No. 12711 (November).

Sanchez, Marcelo (2005). "Is Time Ripe for a Currency Union in Emerging East Asia? The Role of Monetary Stabilization." ECB Working Paper No. 567 (December).

Sato, Kyotaka and Zhaoyong Zhang (2006). "Real Output Co-movements in East Asia: Any Evidence for a Monetary Union?" *The World Economy* 29(12): 1671–1689.

Shin, Kwanho and Chan-Hyun Sohn (2006). "Trade and Financial Integration in East Asia: Effects on Co-movements." *The World Economy* 29(12): 1649–1669.

Suh, Hyun-Deok (2005). "Interest Arbitrage Theory and Capital Movement in Korea." *Review of Foreign Exchange and International Finance* 5: 56–79.

Van Ypersele, Jacques (1985). *The European Monetary System: Origins, Operation and Outlook.* Chicago and London: St. James Press.

Watanabe, Shingo and Masanobu Ogura (2006). "How Far Apart Are Two ACUs from Each Other? Asian Currency Unit and Asian Currency Union." Bank of Japan Working Paper Series No. 06-E-20 (November).

Williamson, John (1999). "The Case for a Common Basket Peg for East Asian Currencies." In Stefan Collignon and Jean Pisani-Ferry (eds.), *Exchange Rate Policies in Emerging Asian Countries* 327–343. London: Routledge.

Williamson, John (2000). *Exchange Rate Regimes for Emerging Markets: Reviving the Intermediate Option.* Policy Analyses in International Economics (60), Institute for International Economics, Washington D.C.

Williamson, John (2005). "A Currency Basket for East Asia, Not Just China." Institute for International Economics, *Policy Briefs in International Economics* no. PB05-1 (August).

Woo, Wing Thye (2007). "What Form Should an Asian Economic Union Take?" *Japan Economic Currents* 67(November): 1–8.

Xinpeng, Xu (2004). "An East Asian Monetary Union?" Hong Kong Polytechnic University. Manuscript.

Xu, Ning (2004). "Monetary Union in Asia." University of Leuven. Manuscript.

Yoshitomi, Masaru (2007). "Global Imbalances and East Asian Monetary Cooperation." In Duck-Koo Chung and Barry Eichengreen (eds.), *Toward an East Asian Exchange Rate Regime* 22–47. Washington, D.C.: Brookings Institution.

Yu, Yongding (1997). "Some Problems with the Pattern of China's International Balance of Payments." *Journal of World Economy and Politics* 10: 18–23 [in Chinese].

Index